ABRAHAM LINCOLN
WAS HE A CHRISTIAN?

by
John Eleazer Remsburg

THE CONFEDERATE
REPRINT COMPANY
☆   ☆   ☆   ☆
WWW.CONFEDERATEREPRINT.COM

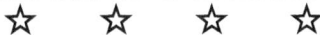

Abraham Lincoln: Was He a Christian?
by John Eleazer Remsburg

Originally Published in 1893
by The Truth Seeker Company
New York

Reprint Edition © 2016
The Confederate Reprint Company
Post Office Box 2027
Toccoa, Georgia 30577
www.confederatereprint.com

Cover and Interior Design by
Magnolia Graphic Design
www.magnoliagraphicdesign.com

ISBN-13: 978-0692729991
ISBN-10: 0692729992

PREFACE

☆　☆　☆　☆

Almost immediately after the remains of America's most illustrious son were laid to rest at Springfield, one of his biographers put forward the claim that he was a devout believer in Christianity. The claim was promptly denied by the dead statesman's friends, but only to be renewed again, and again denied. And thus for a quarter of a century the question of Abraham Lincoln's religious belief has been tossed like a battledoor from side to side.

As a result of this controversy, thousands have become interested in a subject that otherwise might have excited but little interest. This is the writer's apology for collecting the testimony of more than one hundred witnesses, and devoting more than two hundred pages to the question, "Was Lincoln a Christian?"

About few other men has so much been written as about Abraham Lincoln; while no other American's life has engaged the pens of so many biographers. A thousand volumes record his name and refer to his deeds. In a hundred of these he is the central figure. Nearly a score of elaborate biographies of him have been written. As many more books pertaining wholly to his life, his martyrdom, and his character have been published. Of the many works on Lincoln which the writer has consulted in the preparation of this volume, the following deserve to be mentioned: Nicolay and Hay's *Life of Lincoln*, Herndon and Weik's *Life of Lincoln*, Lamon's *Life of Lincoln*, Holland's *Life of Lincoln*, Arnold's *Life of Lincoln*, Raymond's *Life of Lincoln*, Stoddard's *Life of Lincoln*, Barrett's *Life of Lincoln*, *Every-Day Life of Lincoln*, Arnold's *Lincoln and Slavery*, Carpenter's *Six Months at the White House with Lincoln*, *Reminiscences of Lincoln*, *Anecdotes of Lincoln*, *Lincolniana*, *The President's Words*, *The Martyr's Monument*, *Tribute of the Nations to Lincoln*, *Lincoln Memorial* and *Lincoln Memorial Album*.

The testimony concerning Lincoln's religious belief presented in this volume has been derived chiefly from three sources. 1. A part of it has been gathered from the works above named. In a single volume is published for the first time matter which heretofore was only to be found scattered through numerous volumes, some of them inaccessible to the general reader. 2. A considerable portion of it has been gleaned from newspapers and periodicals containing statements brought out by this controversy, many of which would otherwise soon be lost or forgotten. 3. A very large share of it has been obtained by the writer from personal friends of Lincoln; and when we realize how rapidly those who lived and moved with him are passing away – that ere long none of them will remain to testify – the importance of this evidence can hardly be overestimated.

The writer believes that he has fully established the negative of the proposition that forms the title of his book. He does not expect to silence the claims of the affirmative; but he has furnished an arsenal of facts whereby these claims may be exposed and refuted as often as made.

This effort to prove that Lincoln was not a Christian will be condemned by many as an attempt to fasten a stain upon this great man's character. But the demonstration and perpetuation of this fact will only add to his greatness. It will show that he was in advance of his generation. The fame of Abraham Lincoln belongs not to this age alone, but will endure for all time. The popular faith is transient and must perish. It is unpopular now to reject Christianity, but the day is fast approaching when to accept its dogmas will be considered an evidence of human weakness. To perpetuate the claim that Lincoln was a Christian is to perpetuate an idea that in a future age will lessen the luster of his name.

It will be urged by some that the intent and purpose of

this work is solely to promote the interests of Freethought. But it is not. The writer advocates no cause that requires the prestige of a great name to make it respectable. The cause that requires the indorsement of the great to sustain it is not worthy to survive. He has prosecuted this investigation, not in the interest of any belief or creed, but in the interest of truth; and truth is certainly as high as any creed, even if that creed be true. In proving Lincoln a disbeliever he does not presume to have proved Christianity false, or Freethought true; but he has shown that some Christians are not honest, and that an honest man may be a Freehinker.

Atchison, Kansas, April, 1893.

CONTENTS

☆ ☆ ☆ ☆

CHAPTER NINE:
Testimony of Lamon's Witnesses – Concluded

CHAPTER TEN:
Testimony of Lincoln's Relatives and Intimate Associates

CHAPTER ELEVEN:
Testimony of Friends and Acquaintances of Lincoln Who Knew Him in Illinois

CHAPTER TWELVE:
Testimony of Friends and Acquaintances of Lincoln Who Knew Him in Washington

CHAPTER THIRTEEN:
Other Testimony and Opinions

CHAPTER FOURTEEN:
Evidence Gathered From Lincoln's Letters, Speeches, and Conversations

CHAPTER FIFTEEN:
Recapitulation and Conclusion

INTRODUCTION

☆ ☆ ☆ ☆

Was Abraham Lincoln a Christian? Many confidently believe and earnestly contend that he was; others as confidently believe and as earnestly contend that he was not.

Before attempting to answer this question, let us define what constitutes a Christian. A Christian is one who, in common with the adherents of nearly all the religions of mankind, believes, 1. In the existence of a God; 2. In the immortality of the soul. As distinguished from the adherents of other religions, he believes, 1. That the Bible is a revelation from God to man; 2. That Jesus Christ was the miraculously begotten Son of God. He also believes in various other doctrines peculiar to Christianity, the chief of which are, 1. The fall of man; 2. The atonement.

Those who in nominally Christian countries reject the dogmas of Christianity are denominated Infidels, Freethinkers, Liberals, Rationalists, unbelievers, disbelievers, skeptics, etc. These Infidels, Freethinkers, represent various phases of belief among which are, 1. Deists, who affirm the existence of a God and the immortality of the soul; 2. Atheist who deny the existence of a God, and, generally, the soul's immortality; 3. Agnostics, who neither affirm nor deny these doctrines.

The following are the religious views Lincoln is said to have held as presented by those who affirm that he was a Christian:

1. He believed in the existence of a God, and accepted the Christian conception of this Being.

2. He believed in the immortality of the soul, and in the Christian doctrine of the resurrection.

3. He believed that the Bible is a revelation from God –

1

the only revealed will of God.

4. He believed in the divinity of Christ – believed that Christ is God.

5. He believed in the efficacy of prayer, and was accustomed to pray himself.

6. He believed in the doctrine of experimental religion, and had experienced a change of heart.

7. Although he never united with any church, he was contemplating such a step at the time of his assassination.

8. The church with which he would have united, we are led to infer, was the Presbyterian.

The following is a statement of the theological opinions of Lincoln as understood by those who deny that he was a Christian:

1. In regard to a Supreme Being he entertained at times Agnostic and even Atheistic opinions. During the later years of his life, however, he professed a sort of Deistic belief, but he did not accept the Christian or anthropomorphic conception of a Deity.

2. So far as the doctrine of immortality is concerned, he was an Agnostic.

3. He did not believe in the Christian doctrine of the inspiration of the Scriptures. He believed that Burns and Paine were as much inspired as David and Paul.

4. He did not believe in the doctrine of Christ's divinity. He affirmed that Jesus was either the son of Joseph and Mary, or the illegitimate son of Mary.

5. He did not believe in the doctrine of a special creation.

6. He believed in the theory of Evolution, so far as this theory had been developed in his time.

7. He did not believe in miracles and special providences. He believed that all things are governed by immutable laws, and that miracles and special providences, in the evangelical sense of these terms, are impossible.

9. He rejected the doctrine of total, or inherent depravity. He repudiated the doctrine of vicarious atonement.

10. He condemned the doctrine of forgiveness for sin.

11. He opposed the doctrine of future rewards and punishments.

12. He denied the doctrine of the freedom of the will.

13. He did not believe in the efficacy of prayer as understood by orthodox Christians.

14. He indorsed, for the most part, the criticisms of Thomas Paine on the Bible and Christianity, and accepted, to a great extent, the theological and humanitarian views of Theodore Parker.

15. He wrote a book (which was suppressed) against the Bible and Christianity.

16. His connection with public affairs prevented him from giving prominence to his religious opinions during the later years of his life, but his earlier views concerning the unsoundness of the Christian system of religion never underwent any material change, and he died, as he had lived, an unbeliever.

CHAPTER ONE
Christian Testimony
☆　☆　☆　☆

Dr. J.G. Holland – Hon. Newton Bateman – Rev. J.A. Reed
Rev. James Smith, D.D. – N.W. Edwards – Thomas Lewis
Noah Brooks – Rev. Byron Sunderland, D.D. – Rev. Dr. Miner
Rev. Dr. Gurley – Hon. I.N. Arnold – F.B. Carpenter
Isaac Hawley – Rev. Mr. Willets – A Pious Nurse
Western Christian Advocate – An Illinois Clergyman
Rev. J.H. Barrows, D.D. – Rev. Francis Vinton, D.D.1
Bishop Simpson

In confirmation of the claim that Lincoln was a Christian, the following evidence has been adduced:

Dr. J.G. Holland

President Lincoln died on the 15th of April, 1865. In the same year, the *Life of Abraham Lincoln*, written by Dr. J.G. Holland, appeared. In the fields of poetry and fiction, and as a magazine writer, Dr. Holland had achieved an enviable reputation. His *Life of Lincoln* was written in his usually entertaining style and secured a wide circulation. He affirmed that Lincoln was a Christian, and by means of this work, and through *Scribner's Magazine*, of which he was for many years the editor, contributed more than any other person to render a belief in this claim popular. Referring to Lincoln's administration, Dr. Holland says:

The power of a true-hearted Christian man, in perfect sympathy with a true-hearted Christian people, was Mr. Lincoln's power. Open on one side of his nature to all descending influences from him to whom he prayed, and open on the other to all ascending influences from the people whom he served, he aimed simply to do his duty to God and man. Acting rightly he acted greatly. While he took care of deeds fashioned by a purely ideal standard, God took care of results. Moderate, frank, truthful, gentle, forgiving, loving, just, Mr. Lincoln will always be remembered as eminently a Christian President; and the almost immeasurably great results which he had the privilege of achieving were due to the fact that he was a Christian President.[1]

Hon. Newton Bateman

Dr. Holland's claim rests chiefly upon a confession which Lincoln is said to have made to Newton Bateman in 1860. During the Presidential campaign Lincoln occupied the Executive Chamber at the State House. Mr. Bateman was Superintendent of Public Instruction at the time, had his office in the same building, and was frequently in Lincoln's room. The conversation in which Lincoln is alleged to have expressed a belief in Christianity is thus related in Holland's *Life of Lincoln*:

> On one of these occasions Mr. Lincoln took up a book containing a careful canvass of the city of Springfield in which he lived, showing the candidate for whom each citizen had declared it his intention to vote in the approaching election. Mr. Lincoln's friends had, doubtless at his own request, placed the result of the canvass in his hands. This was toward the close of October, and only a few days before the election. Calling Mr. Bateman to a seat at his side, having previously locked all the doors, he said: "Let us look over this book. I wish particularly to see how the ministers of Springfield are going to vote." The leaves were turned, one by one, and as the names were examined Mr. Lincoln frequently asked if this one and that were not a minister, or an elder, or the member of such or such a church, and sadly expressed his surprise on receiving an affirmative answer. In that manner

---

1. *Life of Lincoln*, page 542.

they went through the book, and then he closed it and sat silently and for some minutes regarding a memorandum in pencil which lay before him. At length he turned to Mr. Bateman, with a face full of sadness, and said: "Here are twenty-three ministers, of different denominations, and all of them are against me but three; and here are a great many prominent members of the churches, a very large majority of whom are against me. Mr. Bateman, I am not a Christian – God knows I would be one – but I have carefully read the Bible, and I do not so understand this book;" and he drew from his bosom a pocket New Testament. "These men well know," he continued, "that I am for freedom in the territories, freedom everywhere as far as the Constitution and laws will permit, and that my opponents are for slavery. They know this and yet, with this book in their hands, in the light of which human bondage cannot live a moment, they are going to vote against me. I do not understand it at all."

Here Mr. Lincoln paused – paused for long minutes – his features surcharged with emotion. Then he rose and walked up and down the room in the effort to retain or regain his self-possession. Stopping at last, he said, with a trembling voice and his cheeks wet with tears: "I know there is a God and that he hates injustice and slavery. I see the storm coming, and I know that his hand is in it. If he has a place for me – and I think he has – I believe I am ready. I am nothing, but truth is everything. I know I am right, for Christ teaches it, and Christ is God."

The effect of this conversation upon the mind of Mr. Bateman, a Christian gentleman whom Mr. Lincoln profoundly respected, was to convince him that Mr. Lincoln had, in his quiet way, found a path to the Christian standpoint – that he had found God, and rested on the eternal truth of God. As the two men were about to separate, Mr. Bateman remarked: "I have not supposed that you were accustomed to think so much upon this class of subjects. Certainly your friends generally are ignorant of the sentiments you have expressed to me." He replied quickly: "I know they are. I am obliged to appear different to them; but I think more upon these subjects than upon all others, and I have done so for years; and I am willing that you should know it."[2]

---

2. *Life of Lincoln*, pp. 236-239.

Rev. J. A. Reed

In 1872, seven years after the publication of Holland's work, Lamon's *Life of Abraham Lincoln* was published. In this work the statements of Holland and Bateman concerning Lincoln's religious belief are disputed, and the testimony of numerous witnesses cited to prove that he lived and died a disbeliever. Soon after Lamon's book was published, the Rev. J. A. Reed, a Presbyterian clergyman, of Springfield, Ill., delivered a lecture in which he attempted to refute or modify the evidence of Lamon's witnesses and prove that Lincoln died a Christian. He admitted that Lincoln was an Infidel up to 1848 and possibly as late as 1862, but endeavored to show that previous to his death he changed his views and became a Christian. The following extracts present the salient points in his discourse:

> Having shown what claims Mr. Lamon's book has to being the "only fair and reliable history" of Mr. Lincoln's life and views, and of what "trustworthy materials" it is composed, I shall now give the testimony I have collected to establish what has ever been the public impression, that Mr. Lincoln was in his later life, and at the time of his death, a firm believer in the truth of the Christian religion. The Infidelity of his earlier life is not so much to be wondered at, when we consider the poverty of his early religious instruction and the peculiar influences by which he was surrounded.
>
> It does not appear that he had ever seen, much less read, a work on the evidences of Christianity till his interview with Rev. Dr. Smith in 1848. We hear of him as reading Paine, Voltaire, and Theodore Parker, but nothing on the other side.
>
> While it is to be regretted that Mr. Lincoln was not spared to indicate his religious sentiments by a profession of his faith in accordance with the institutions of the Christian religion, yet it is very clear that he had this step in view, and was seriously contemplating it, as a sense of its fitness and an apprehension of his duty grew upon him.

In support of his claims, Dr. Reed presents the testimony of Rev. Dr. Smith, Ninian W. Edwards, Thomas Lewis, Noah Brooks, Rev. Dr. Sunderland, Rev. Dr. Miner, and Rev. Dr. Gurley.

Rev. James Smith, D.D.

The Rev. James Smith was for many years pastor of the First Presbyterian Church of Springfield. Lincoln formed his acquaintance soon after he located there, remained on friendly terms with him, and with Mrs. Lincoln frequently attended his church. Dr. Smith was one of the three Springfield clergymen who supported Lincoln for President in 1860, and in recognition of his friendship and fidelity, he received the consulship at Dundee. Dr. Reed quotes from a letter to W.H. Herndon, dated East Cainno, Scotland, January 24, 1867, in which Dr. Smith says:

> It is a very easy matter to prove that while I was pastor of the First Presbyterian Church of Springfield, Mr. Lincoln did avow his belief in the divine authority and inspiration of the scriptures, and I hold that it is a matter of the last importance not only to the present, but all future generations of the great Republic, and to all advocates of civil and religious liberty throughout the world that this avowal on his part, and the circumstances attending it, together with very interesting incidents illustrative of the excellence of his character, in my possession, should be made known to the public. . . . It was my honor to place before Mr. Lincoln arguments designed to prove the divine authority and inspiration of the scriptures accompanied by the arguments of Infidel objectors in their own language. To the arguments on both sides Mr. Lincoln gave a most patient, impartial, and searching investigation. To use his own language, he examined the arguments as a lawyer who is anxious to reach the truth investigates testimony. The result was the announcement by himself that the argument in favor of the divine authority and inspiration of the Scriptures was unanswerable.

Hon. Ninian W. Edwards

Ninian W. Edwards, a brother-in-law of Lincoln writes as follows:

Springfield, Dec. 24th, 1872.

Rev. Jas. A. Reed:

Dear Sir –

A short time after the Rev. Dr. Smith became pastor of the First Presbyterian church in this city, Mr. Lincoln said to me, "I have been reading a work of Dr. Smith on the evidences of Christianity, and have heard him preach and converse on the subject, and I am now convinced of the truth of the Christian religion."

Yours truly,

N. W. Edwards.

Thomas Lewis

In corroboration of Mr. Edwards's statement, Thomas Lewis, of Springfield, Ill., testifies as follows:

Springfield, Jan. 6th, 1873.

Rev. J. A. Reed:

Dear Sir –

Not long after Dr. Smith came to Springfield, and I think very near the time of his son's death, Mr. Lincoln said to me, that when on a visit somewhere, he had seen and partially read a work of Dr. Smith on the evidences of Christianity which had led him to change his views about the Christian religion; that he would like to get that work to finish the reading of it, and also to make the acquaintance of Dr. Smith. I was an elder in Dr. Smith's church, and took Dr. Smith to Mr. Lincoln's office and introduced him; and Dr. Smith gave Mr. Lincoln a copy of his book, as I know, at his own request.

Yours etc.,

Thos. Lewis.

Noah Brooks

Noah Brooks, a newspaper correspondent of New York, and the author of a biography of Lincoln gives the following testimony:

New York, Dec. 31, 1872.

Rev. J.A. Reed,

My Dear Sir:

In addition to what has appeared from my pen, I will state that I have had many conversations with Mr. Lincoln, which were more or less of a religious character, and while I never tried to draw anything like a statement of his views from him, yet he freely expressed himself to me as having "a hope of blessed immortality through Jesus Christ." His view seemed to settle so naturally around that statement that I considered no other necessary. His language seemed not that of an inquirer, but of one who had a prior settled belief in the fundamental doctrines of the Christian religion. Once or twice speaking to me of the change which had come upon him, he said, while he could not fix any definite time, yet it was after he came here, and I am very positive that in his own mind he identified it with about the time of Willie's death. He said, too, that after he went to the White House he kept up the habit of daily prayer. Sometimes he said it was only ten words, but those ten words he had. There is no possible reason to suppose that Mr. Lincoln would ever deceive me as to his religious sentiments. In many conversations with him, I absorbed the firm conviction that Mr. Lincoln was at heart a Christian man, believed in the Savior, and was seriously considering the step which would formally connect him with the visible church on earth. Certainly, any suggestion as to Mr. Lincoln's skepticism or Infidelity, to me who knew him intimately from 1862 till the time of his death, is a monstrous fiction – a shocking perversion.

Yours truly,

Noah Brooks.

Rev. Byron Sunderland, D.D.

Mr. Reed presents a lengthy letter from the Rev. Byron Sunderland, of Washington, dated Nov. 15, 1872. Dr. Sunderland in company with a party of friends visited the President in the autumn of 1862. In this letter he says:

After some conversation, in which he seemed disposed to have his joke and fun, he settled down to a serious consideration of the subject before his mind, and for one half-hour poured forth a volume of the deepest Christian philosophy I ever heard.

Rev. Dr. Miner

The Rev. Dr. Miner, who met Lincoln in Washington, says:

All that was said during that memorable afternoon I spent alone with that great and good man is engraven too deeply on my memory ever to be effaced. I felt certain of this fact, that if Mr. Lincoln was not really an experimental Christian, he was acting like one. He was doing his duty manfully, and looking to God for help in time of need and, like the immortal Washington, he believed in the efficacy of prayer, and it was his custom to read the Scriptures and pray himself.

Rev. P.D. Gurlet, D.D.

While in Washington, Lincoln with his family attended the Presbyterian church of which the Rev. Dr. Gurley was pastor. Mr. Reed cites the following as the testimony of Dr. Gurley in regard to the alleged Infidelity of Lincoln:

I do not believe a word of it. It could not have been true of him while here, for I have had frequent and intimate conversations with him on the subject of the Bible and the Christian religion, when he could have had no motive to deceive me, and I considered him sound not only on the truth of the Christian religion but on all its fundamental doctrine and teachings. And more than that, in the latter days of his chastened and weary life, after the death of his son Willie, and his visit to the battle-field of Gettysburg, he said, with tears in his eyes, that he had lost confidence in everything but God, and that he now believed his heart was changed, and that he loved the Savior, and, if he was not deceived in himself, it was his intention soon to make a profession of religion.

Hon. Isaac N. Arnold

One of the most ardent friends and admirers of Abraham Lincoln was Isaac N. Arnold, for several years a member of Congress from Illinois. Mr. Arnold wrote a work on *Lincoln and Slavery*, and a *Life of Lincoln* which was published in 1885. Lincoln's religious views are thus described by Mr. Arnold:

> No more reverent Christian than he ever sat in the Executive chair, not excepting Washington. He was by nature religious; full of religious sentiment. The veil between him and the supernatural was very thin. It is not claimed that he was orthodox. For creeds and dogmas he cared little. But in the great fundamental principles of religion, of the Christian religion, he was a firm believer. Belief in the existence of God, in the immortality of the soul, in the Bible as the revelation of God to man, in the efficacy and duty of prayer, in reverence toward the Almighty, and in love and charity to man, was the basis of his religion. . . .
>
> His reply to the Negroes of Baltimore when they, in 1864, presented him with a magnificent Bible, ought to silence forever those who charge him with unbelief. He said, "In regard to the Great Book I have only to say that it is the best gift which God has given to man. All the good from the Savior of the world is communicated through this book. . . ."
>
> His faith in a Divine Providence began at his mother's knee, and ran through all the changes his life. Not orthodox, not a man of creeds, he was a man of simple trust in God.[3]

F.B. Carpenter

Mr. Carpenter, the artist, in his popular book entitled, *Six Months in the White House With Abraham Lincoln*, uses the following language: "I would scarcely have called Mr. Lincoln a religious man – and yet I believe him to have been sincere Christian."[4]

---

3. *Life of Lincoln*, pp. 446, 447, 448..
4. *Six Months in the White House With Abraham Lincoln*, p. 185.

Isaac Hawley

In the spring of 1887, in going from Springfield to Havana, I met Isaac Hawley, one of the early settlers of Illinois, and who for nearly twenty years resided within a few blocks of Lincoln in Springfield. In answer to the question, "Was Lincoln a Christian?" Mr. Hawley replied: "I believe that Lincoln was a Christian, and that he was God's chosen instrument to perform the mighty work he did."

Rev. Mr. Willets

The Rev. Mr. Willets, of Brooklyn, N.Y., is credited with the following statement concerning Lincoln's reputed conversion. The information it contains was obtained, it is said, from a lady of Mr. Willets's acquaintance who met Lincoln in Washington:

> The President, it seemed, had been much impressed with the devotion and earnestness of purpose manifested by the lady, and on one occasion, after she had discharged the object of her visit, he said to her: "Mrs. —, I have formed a high opinion of your Christian character, and now, as we are alone, I have a mind to ask you to give me, in brief, your idea of what constitutes a true religious experience." The lady replied at some length, stating that, in her judgment, it consisted of a conviction of one's own sinfulness and weakness, and personal need of a Savior for strength and support; that views of mere doctrine might and would differ, but when one was really brought to feel his need of divine help, and to seek the aid of the Holy Spirit for strength and guidance, it was satisfactory evidence of his having been born again. This was the substance of her reply. When she had concluded, Mr. Lincoln was very thoughtful for a few moments. He at length said, very earnestly, "If what you have told me is really a correct view of this great subject I think I can say with sincerity that I hope I am a Christian."[5]

---

5. *Anecdotes of Lincoln*, pp. 166, 167.

A Pious Nurse

A pious lady, who served in the capacity of a hospital nurse at Washington, and who sometimes visited the White House, testifies to Lincoln's belief in the efficacy of prayer. The incident narrated occurred while a battle was in progress. The report says:

> The possibility of defeat depressed him greatly but the lady told him he must trust, and that he could at least pray. "Yes," said he, and taking up a Bible, he started for his room. Could all the people of the nation have overheard the earnest petition that went up from that inner chamber as it reached the ears of the nurse, they would have fallen upon their knees with tearful and reverential sympathy.[6]

Western Christian Advocate

Soon after the close of the war, the *Western Christian Advocate*, the leading Christian journal of the West, published the following:

> On the day of the receipt of the capitulation of Lee, as we learn from a friend intimate with the late President Lincoln, the cabinet meeting was held an hour earlier than usual. Neither the President nor any member was able, for a time, to give utterance to his feelings. At the suggestion of Mr. Lincoln all dropped on their knees, and offered in silence and in tears their humble and heartfelt acknowledgment to the Almighty for the triumph he had granted to the national cause.

The above is quoted by Raymond and other biographers of Lincoln.

An Illinois Clergyman

In the *Lincoln Memorial Album* appears what is reported

---

6. *Anecdotes of Lincoln*, p. 120.

to be Lincoln's "Reply to an Illinois Clergyman":

> "When I left Springfield I asked the people to pray for me. I was not a Christian. When I buried my son, the severest trial of my life, I was not a Christian. But when I went to Gettysburg, and saw the graves of thousands of our soldiers, I then and there consecrated myself to Christ. Yes, I do love Jesus."[7]

Rev. John H. Barrows

In the *Lincoln Memorial Album*, Dr. J. H. Barrows contributes an article on "The Religious Aspects of Abraham Lincoln's Career," from which I quote as follows:

> In the anxious uncertainties of the great war, he gradually rose to the heights where Jehovah became to him the sublimest of realities, the ruler of nations. When he wrote his immortal Proclamation, invoked upon it not only "the considerate judgment of mankind," but "the gracious favor of Almighty God." When darkness gathered over the brave armies fighting for the nation's life, this strong man in the early morning knelt and wrestled in prayer with him who holds in his hand the fate of empires. When the clouds lifted above the carnage of Gettyburg, he gave his heart to the Lord Jesus Christ. When he pronounced his matchless oration on the chief battlefield of the war, he gave expression to the resolve that "this nation, under God, should have a new birth of freedom." And when he wrote his last Inaugural Address, he gave to it the lofty religious tone of an old Hebrew psalm.[8]

Rev. Francis Vinton, D.D.

This clergyman, a resident of New York, and stranger to Lincoln, visited the White House in 1862, it is claimed, and indulged in an argument and exhortation, the effect of which was to convert the President to a belief in the Christian doctrine of

---

7. *Lincoln Memorial Album*, p. 366.

8. *Ibid.*, p. 508.

the resurrection and the immortality of the soul. During the interview, Lincoln, it is reported, fell upon the neck of his clerical visitor and wept like a child.

Before retiring, Dr. Vinton said: "I have a sermon upon this subject which I think might interest you." "Mr. Lincoln," the report continues, "begged him to send it at an early day, thanking him repeatedly for his cheering and hopeful words. The sermon was sent, and read over and over by the President, who caused a copy to be made for his own private use before it was returned."[9]

Bishop Simpson

The most eminent Methodist divine of that period was Bishop Simpson. During the war his commanding influence and rare eloquence did much to secure for the Union cause the united support of Northern Methodists. Lincoln appreciated the services of the distinguished divine, and they became warm friends. When the remains of the President were conveyed to their final resting-place at Springfield, Bishop Simpson was selected to deliver the funeral oration. Alluding to the religious phase of Lincoln's character, he spoke as follows:

> As a ruler, I doubt if any President has ever shown such trust in God, or in public documents so frequently referred to divine aid. Often did he remark to friends and to delegations that his hope for our success rested in his conviction that God would bless our efforts because we were trying to right.[10]

---

9. *Anecdotes of Lincoln*, pp. 107, 108.

10. *Lincoln and Slavery*, p. 673.

CHAPTER TWO
Review of Christian Testimony –
Holland and Bateman
☆ ☆ ☆ ☆

Character of Holland's Life of Lincoln – Bateman Interview
Inconsistency and Untruthfulness of its Statements
Holland's Subsequent Modification and Final Abandonment
of His Original Claims.

In the preceding chapter has been presented the Christian side of this question. It has been presented fully and fairly. Even the Christian claimant must admit that it is the longest and most complete array of testimony that has yet been published in support of his claim. This evidence is explicit and apparently conclusive. To attempt its refutation may seem presumptuous. And yet, in the face of all this evidence, the writer does not hesitate to declare that Abraham Lincoln was not a Christian, and pledge himself to refute the statements of these witnesses by a volume of testimony that is irresistible and overwhelming.

Before introducing this testimony the evidence already adduced will be reviewed. This evidence may properly be grouped into three divisions: 1. The testimony of Holland and Bateman; 2. The testimony of Reed and his witnesses; 3. The testimony of Arnold and the miscellaneous evidence remaining. Holland's *Life of Lincoln*, from a literary point of view, is a work of more than ordinary merit. It possesses a beauty of diction and an intellectual vigor seldom surpassed; but as an authority it is unreliable. Like Weems's *Life of Washington*, it is simply a biographical romance founded upon fact, but paying little regard to facts in presenting the details. Following the natural bent of Christian biographers, Holland parades the subject of his work as a model of Christian piety. He knew that this was false; for, while he was unacquainted with Lincoln, he had been apprised of his unbelief – had been repeatedly told of it before he wrote his biography. But this did not deter him from asserting the contrary. He knew that if he stated the facts the clergy would condemn his book. They needed the influence of Lincoln's great name to support their crumbling creed, and would have it at any sacrifice, particularly when its possession required no greater sacrifice than truth. Holland was equal to the emergency. When one of Lincoln's friends in Springfield suggested that the less said about his religious views the better, he promptly replied: "Oh, never mind; I'll fix that." And he did. With dramatic embellishments, he presented to the delight of the orthodox world the now famous, or rather infamous, Bateman interview.

The publication of this story produced a profound sensation among the personal friends of the dead President. It revealed to them the unpleasant fact, assuming Holland's account to be correct, either that Newton Bateman, who had hitherto borne the reputation of being a man of veracity, was an unscrupulous liar, or that Abraham Lincoln, whose reputation for honesty and candor, long anterior to 1860, had become proverbial, was a consummate hypocrite; and loath as they were to believe the former, they rejected with disdain the latter.

Referring to this story, Lamon, in his *Life of Lincoln*, says: "There is no dealing with Mr. Bateman except by a flat contradiction. Perhaps his memory was treacherous or his imagination led him astray, or, peradventure, he thought a fraud no harm if it gratified the strong desire of the public for proofs of Mr. Lincoln's orthodoxy."[1]

While Bateman undoubtedly misrepresented Lincoln in his account of their conversation – for it is not denied that he had an interview with Lincoln – it is quite probable that he did not to the extent represented by Holland. Bateman doubtless exagger-

---

1. *Life of Lincoln*, p. 501.

ated the affair, and Holland magnified Bateman's report of it. In an article originally published in the Index, and subsequently quoted by Lamon, Lincoln's law partner, Mr. Herndon, says:

> I doubt whether Mr. Bateman said in full what is recorded there. I doubt a great deal of it. I know the whole story is untrue – untrue in substance, untrue in fact and spirit. As soon as the [Holland's] *Life of Lincoln* was out, on reading that part here referred to, I instantly sought Mr. Bateman and found him in his office. I spoke to him politely and kindly, and he spoke to me in the same manner. I said substantially to him that Mr. Holland, in order to make Mr. Lincoln a technical Christian, made him a hypocrite; and so his *Life of Lincoln* quite plainly says. I loved Mr. Lincoln and was mortified, if not angry, to see him made hypocrite. I cannot now detail what Mr. Bateman said as it was a private conversation, and I am forbidden to make use of it in public. If some good gentleman can only get the seal of secrecy removed I can show what was said and done. On my word, the world may take it for granted that Holland is wrong – that he does not state Mr. Lincoln's views correctly.[2]

In a lecture on "Lincoln's Religion," delivered in Springfield in 1874, alluding to the same subject Mr. Herndon says:

> My notes of our conversation bear date December 3, 12, and 28, 1865. Our conversations were private, I suppose. However, I can say this much: that Mr. Bateman expressly told me Mr. Lincoln was, in the conversation related in Holland, talking politics and not religion, nor Christianity, nor morals, as such. I have persistently dogged Mr. Bateman for the privilege of publishing my notes, or to give me a letter explaining what Mr. Lincoln did say, so that I might make known the facts of the case. Mr. Bateman has as stoutly refused.

Dr. Bateman finally permitted Mr. Herndon to make public a letter, marked "confidential," which he had written Mr. Herndon in 1867. In this letter Bateman says:

---

2. Lamon's *Life of Lincoln*, p. 496.

He [Lincoln] was applying the principles of moral and religious truth to the duties of the hour, the condition of the country, and the conduct of public men – ministers of the gospel. I had no thought of orthodoxy or heterodoxy, Unitarianism, Trinitarianism, or any other ism, during the whole conversation, and I don't suppose or believe he had.

Had Lincoln made the confession he is reported to have made, this would have suggested to Mr. Bateman the idea of his admitted orthodoxy as well as his reputed heterodoxy. Had Lincoln declared that "Christ is God," this would have suggested to him the idea of Trinitarianism. It will be seen, even from this letter, that instead of talking theology and professing a belief in Christianity, he was talking politics and denouncing the intolerance and bigotry of Christian ministers.

Dr. Bateman privately asserts that he was not correctly reported, that Holland's version of the interview "is colored." It is to be regretted that he had not the courage to state this fact to the public, and his plea, "My aversion to publicity in such matters is intense," is a poor apology for refusing do so.

As previously intimated, this story is probably founded on fact and has an element of truth in it. Lincoln and Bateman had a political interview, and the object of this interview was the examination and discussion of the list of Springfield voters. This list revealed the fact that twenty out of twenty-three clergymen and a very large majority of the church-members of Springfield were opposed to Lincoln. The significance of this fact Dr. Holland and Dr. Bateman have apparently overlooked. Why was the church opposed to him? It must have been either because it was opposed to the Republican party, or because he was personally objectionable to the members of that party. His political principles were the principles of his party, his ability was conceded, and his moral character was above reproach. It is fair to assume that the political sentiment of the Christians of Springfield was substantially the political sentiment of Northern Christians generally. Now, was the Northern Church overwhelmingly in favor of the extension of slavery? Were eighty-seven per cent. of Northern Christians Democrats? Or did the Christians of Springfield oppose Lincoln because he was an Infidel?

Holland makes Bateman affirm that Lincoln "drew from his bosom a pocket New Testament." It is generally believed by Lincoln's friends that he did not have a New Testament, that the only book used in the interview was the book containing the list of Springfield voters. One of them says: "The idea that Mr. Lincoln carried the New Testament or Bible in his bosom or boots, to draw on his opponents in debate, is ridiculous." It is possible, however, that there was a New Testament in the room, and that Lincoln used it to enforce an argument. Indeed, there is internal evidence in the story, aside from the declaration of Bateman, that such was the case. The central idea in his political creed – the keynote of his campaigns, both in 1858 and in 1860 – was contained in that memorable passage, "'A house divided against itself cannot stand.' This government cannot endure permanently half slave and half free." The figure quoted was a familiar and powerful one, and Lincoln recognized its force in dealing with the masses. It was taken from the New Testament, and from the words of Christ himself. That he should use it against those Christians who were acting contrary to this well-known truth, is not strange. Immediately after the declaration, "Christ is God," he is reported as saying: "I have told them that a house divided against itself cannot stand, and Christ and reason say the same." This furnishes a solution to the whole story. This shows what he was doing with a New Testament. In connection with this, nothing is more natural than that he should exclaim: "Christ teaches it, and Christ is [their] God!" That he was terribly in earnest, that he was deeply agitated and pained to learn that his Christian neighbors were opposed to him, is not improbable. Thus the incidents of a simple political interview that were natural and reasonable have been perverted to make it appear that he was a Christian. A mere reference to the New Testament and Christ have been twisted into an acknowledgment of their divinity. Bateman himself admits that Lincoln said: "I am not a Christian." Why not accept his statement, then? Why then distort his words and in the face of this positive declaration attempt to prove that he was a Christian? Bateman reports him as modifying the statement by adding: "God knows I would be one." Yes, "God knows I would be one were I convinced that Christianity is true, but not convinced of its truth, I am an unbeliever."

Lincoln is also reported to have said that, in the light of the New Testament, "human bondage can not live a moment." But he did not utter these words. He did not utter them because they are untrue, and none knew this better than himself. He knew that in the light of this book human bondage had lived for nearly two thousand years; he knew that this book was one of the great bulwarks of human slavery; he knew that there was not to be found between its lids a single text condemning slavery, while there were to be found a score of texts sustaining it; he knew that that infamous law, the Fugitive Slave law, received its warrant from this book – that Paul, in the light of its earliest teachings, had returned a fugitive slave to his master.

In this story Lincoln is charged with the grossest hypocrisy. He is declared to have professed a belief in Christ and Christianity, and when Bateman observed that his friends were ignorant of this, he is made to reply: "I know they are. I am obliged to appear different to them." Now, to use Lincoln's own words, "A sane person can no more act without a motive than can there be an effect without a cause," and what possible motive could he have had for such conduct? Supposing that he was base enough to be a hypocrite, what could induce him to lead the world to suppose he was an Infidel if he were not? In the eyes of the more ignorant and bigoted class of Christians, Infidelity is a more heinous crime than murder, and an Infidel is a creature scarcely to be tolerated, much less to be intrusted with a public office. Freethinkers generally detest the dogmas of Christianity as thoroughly as Christians possibly can the principles of Freethought. But free thought and free speech are the leading tenets of their creed. They recognize the fact that we are all the children of circumstances, that our belief is determined by our environments, and while they reject Christianity, they have nothing but charity for those who conscientiously profess it. They may repudiate a bigot, but will not oppose a man merely because he is a Christian. If Lincoln were an Infidel, discretion might urge a concealment of his views; if he were Christian, policy would prompt him to give it as wide a publicity as possible, especially when he rested under the imputation of being a disbeliever. Had he changed his belief and become a convert to Christianity, a knowledge of the fact would not have lost him the support of his friends, even though some of them were Freethinkers; while it would have secured for him a more cordial support from the Republican side of the church, many of whom had been alienated on account of his supposed anti-Christian sentiments. It is hard to believe that Lincoln was a hypocrite; but this story, if true makes him not only a hypocrite but a fool. If he believed in Christianity there can be but one reason advanced for his desiring to keep it a secret – he was ashamed of it.

Holland, in trying to explain away the inconsistencies of this fabrication, repeatedly blunders. In one of his attempts he makes use of the following remarkable language:

> It was one of the peculiarities of Mr. Lincoln to hide these religious experiences from the eyes of the world. . . . They [his friends] did not regard him as a religious man. They had never seen anything but the active lawyer, the keen politician, the jovial, fun-loving companion in Mr. Lincoln. All this department of his life he had kept carefully hidden from them. Why he should say that he was obliged to appear differently to others does not appear; but the fact is a matter of history that he never exposed his own religious life to those who had no sympathy with it. It is doubtful whether the clergymen of Springfield knew anything of these experiences.[3]

What! had the clergymen of Springfield no sympathy with a religious life? A person can utter one falsehood with some degree of plausibility; but when he attempts to verify it by uttering another, he usually trips and falls. The above passage is mere hypocritical cant. It carries with it not only its own refutation, but

---

3. *Life of Lincoln*, pp. 239, 240.

that of the rest of Holland's testimony also. It is the language of the man who is conscious of having stated a falsehood; conscious that there are others who believe it to be a falsehood. He knew that the personal friends of Lincoln all understood him to be a disbeliever. He knew that the church-members of Springfield all entertained the same opinion. He virtually says to these people: "It is true that Lincoln professed to be an Infidel, but he was not; he was a Christian. The fact has been kept a profound secret. Bateman and I have been the sole custodians of this secret, and we now give it to the world."

A Christian writer, apologizing for the absurd and contradictory statements of Holland and Bateman, says, "They aimed at the truth." I do not believe it. It is clearly evident that they aimed at a plausible lie. But in either case they made a bad shot.

In his *Life of Lincoln*, Holland endeavors to convey the impression that Lincoln was always a devout Christian. He declares that even during the years of his early manhood at New Salem, "he was a religious man;" that "he had a deep religious life." When Herndon and Lamon exposed his shameful misrepresentations he retreated from his first position, and in *Scribner's Monthly* wrote as follows:

> What Abraham Lincoln was when he lived at New Salem and wrote an anti-Christian tract (which the friend to whom he showed it somewhat violently but most judiciously put in the fire) is one thing, and it may be necessary for an impartial historian to record it. What he was when he died at Washington with those most Christian words of the Second Inaugural upon his lips, and that most Christian record of five years of patient tenderness and charity behind him, is quite another thing.

He admits that Lincoln was an Infidel in Illinois, but would have us believe that he was a Christian in Washington. He refers to "those most Christian words of the Second Inaugural," and "that most Christian record of five years of patient tenderness and charity." In the Second Inaugural there is not a word affirming a belief in Christianity not a word in reference to Christianity. He mentions God, and quotes from the Bible, but does not intimate that the Bible is God's word. That Christians have a monopoly of "patient tenderness and charity," can hardly be accepted. The history of the church does not confirm this assumption. Many Christians have possessed these virtues. So have the votaries of other religions. These attributes belong to good men everywhere, but they are the distinguishing features of no particular creed.

Smarting under his exposure, with that whining pant so peculiar to the vanquished religionist, Holland finally sent forth this parting wail and virtually abandoned the whole case:

> The question is, not whether Abraham Lincoln was a subscriber to the creeds of orthodoxy, but whether he was a believing, that is to say, a truthful Christian man; not whether he was accustomed to call Jesus Christ "Lord, Lord," but whether he was used to do those things which Jesus Christ exemplified and enforced. He was accustomed, as we know well enough, to speak of an Almighty Father, of whom justice and mercy and sympathy with weak and suffering humanity were characteristic attributes. Who was it that revealed to man a God like this? Who was it that once "showed us the Father and it sufficed us"? Whoever it was that made this revelation to mankind it was of him that this man, even though he knew it not, had learned, and it was his spirit that he acted.[4]

The concluding words of Dr. Holland's testimony, as quoted from his *Life of Lincoln*, are as follows:

> Moderate, frank, truthful, gentle, forgiving, loving, just, Mr. Lincoln will always be remembered eminently a Christian President; and the almost immeasurably great results which he had the privilege of achieving were due to the fact that he was a Christian President.

This prediction and this assumption are false. I change one word and make them grandly true. "Moderate, frank, truthful, gentle, forgiving, loving, just, Mr. Lincoln will always

---

4. *Scribner's Monthly.*

be remembered as eminently a Liberal President; and the almost immeasurably great results which he had the privilege of achieving were due to the fact that he was a Liberal President.

CHAPTER THREE
Review of Christian Testimony –
Reed and His Witnesses
☆ ☆ ☆ ☆

Reed – Smith – Edwards – Lewis – Brooks – Statements of
Edward Smith, and Brooks Compared – Sunderland – Miner
Gurley – Failure of Reed to Establish His Claims

Of the twenty Christian witnesses whose testimony is
given in Chapter One, ten admit that, during a part of his life,
Lincoln was an unbeliever, or Infidel. Of the remaining ten, not
one denies the fact. It is conceded, then, that he was once an
Infidel. Now it is a rule of law that when a certain state or
condition of things is once proven to exist, that state or condition
is presumed to continue to exist until the contrary is proven. If
Lincoln was, at one time, an Infidel, it is fair to assume that he
remained an Infidel, unless it can be shown that he changed his
belief and became a Christian. This Dr. Reed attempts to do.

His lecture, under the caption of "The Later Life and
Religious Sentiments of Abraham Lincoln," will be found in
Scribner's Monthly for July, 1873. The evidence presented by
Lamon had placed Dr. Holland in a most unenviable light. As
Reed's lecture reaffirmed the claim made by Holland, and
brought forward fresh evidence to substantiate the claim, it was
naturally regarded by many Christians as a vindication of
Holland's position, especially by those who had not read Lamon's
work. Holland was particularly pleased at its opportune appear-
ance, and cheerfully gave it a place in his magazine.

Reed's individual testimony proves nothing. He does not

profess to know, from personal knowledge, what Lincoln's religious views were. The object of his lecture was to invalidate, if possible, the testimony of those who affirmed that he died an Infidel, and to present, in addition to what had already been presented by Holland, the testimony of those who affirmed that during the last years of his life he was a Christian. To answer his witnesses is to answer his lecture.

The Rev. Dr. Smith affirms that he converted Lincoln to a belief in *"the divine authority and inspiration of the Scriptures."* It was imperative that he should, for, said he, "It was my honor to place before Mr. Lincoln arguments designed to prove *the divine authority and inspiration of the Scriptures."* As a matter of course, "the result was the announcement by himself that the arguments in favor of *the divine authority and inspiration of the Scriptures* were unanswerable." Consequently, "Mr. Lincoln did avow his belief in *the divine authority and inspiration of the Scriptures."*

Impressed with a deep sense of the gravity and importance of his work, he declares that, "It is a matter of the last importance not only to the present but to all future generations of the great Republic, and to all advocates of civil and religious liberty throughout the world that this avowal on his part, . . . should be made known to the public;" coupled with the more important fact, of course that it was Dr. Smith who did it. It is to be regretted that his waiting until after Lincoln's death to announce it, prevented the convert's Christian friends from tendering their congratulations and extending the hand of fellowship. It is possible that he counseled Dr. Smith not to divulge the secret for fear it might injure his political prospects. Certain it is, his neighbors were ignorant of this remarkable change. When Holland canvassed Springfield, 1865, eager to obtain a morsel of evidence upon which to base his claim that Lincoln was a Christian, he failed to catch even the faintest whisper regarding this alleged conversion.

When Dr. Smith's letter was made public, the Christians of Springfield generally smiled, but said nothing, while unbelievers laughed outright and pronounced it the acme of absurdity. Dr.

Reed read it to his audience and tried to look serious.

Concerning this claim, Lincoln's biographer, Colonel Lamon, says:

> The abilities of this gentleman to discuss such a topic to the edification of a man like Mr. Lincoln seem to have been rather slender; but the chance of converting so distinguished a person inspired him with a zeal which he might not have felt for the salvation of an obscurer soul. Mr. Lincoln listened to his exhortations in silence, apparently respectful, and occasionally sat out his sermons in church with as much patience as other people. Finding these oral appeals unavailing, Mr. Smith composed a heavy tract out of his own head to suit the particular case. "The preparation of that work," says he, "cost me long and arduous labor;" but it does not appear to have been read. Mr. Lincoln took the "work" to his office, laid it down without writing his name on it, and never took it up again to the knowledge of a man who inhabited the office with him, and who saw it lying on the same spot every day for months. Subsequently Mr. Smith drew from Mr. Lincoln an acknowledgment that his argument was unanswerable – not a very high compliment under the circumstances.[1]

The gentleman whom Colonel Lamon refers to as testifying that Lincoln did not read Dr. Smith's book was Lincoln's partner, Mr. Herndon. In his lecture on "Lincoln's Religion," Mr. Herndon says: "Mr. Lincoln received a book from Dr. Smith on Infidelity. He placed it on our law table. He never opened it and never read it to my knowledge."

If Dr. Smith had converted Lincoln, as claimed, is it not reasonable to suppose that he would have joined Dr. Smith's church? Had he been converted, would the clergymen of Springfield have denounced him as an Infidel in 1860? Again, if Dr. Smith's book was so effective as to convert from Infidelity to Christianity as great a mind as Lincoln, why have we not heard more of it? Why has it not been used to convert other Infidels? Was its vitality as an evangelizer exhausted in converting Lincoln?

---

1. *Life of Lincoln*, p. 498.

Mr. Reed was a trifle more successful than Dr. Holland in obtaining witnesses; for while Holland was able to secure but one witness in Illinois, Reed was able to summon two – Ninian Edwards and Thomas Lewis.

The testimony of Mr. Edwards, providing that he was the author of the letter accredited to him, can only be accounted for on the following supposition. Being a believer in Christianity himself, he considered Lincoln's Infidelity a grave defect in his character, and was vexed to see that this controversy had given it such wide publicity. To assist in removing this stain, as he regarded it, from his kinsman's name, he allowed to be published over his signature a statement which, unless his memory was very treacherous, he must have known was untrue.

It may be that Lincoln did change his views in regard to some historical or doctrinal point connected with Christianity, and informed Mr. Edwards and other friends at the time of the fact. He might have changed his opinions on a hundred theological questions without having in the least changed his views in relation to the main or fundamental doctrines of Christianity. An admission concerning some trivial question connected with Christianity has been tortured to convey the idea that he accepted the whole system.

A prominent and respected citizen of Springfield, a gentleman whose name has, as yet, not been mentioned in connection with this controversy, had a conversation with Mr. Edwards relative to this subject, soon after Reed's lecture was published, and, as the result of that conversation, he writes as follows: "Mr. Edwards was not as good a witness on oral examination as he was in print."

The letter of Mr. Edwards is dated Dec. 24, 1872. On Jan. 6, 1873, the letter of Thomas Lewis was written. After two weeks of arduous labor, Reed, it seems, succeeded in finding one witness in Springfield who was prepared to corroborate the testimony of Edwards – Thomas Lewis.

In a lecture on Lincoln which appeared in the *State Register,* of Springfield, Mr. Herndon disposed of this witness as follows:

Mr. Lewis's veracity and integrity in this community need no comment. I have heard good men say they would not believe his word under any circumstances, especially if he were interested. I hate to state this of Tom, but if he will obtrude himself in this discussion, I cannot help but say a word in self-defense. Mr. Lincoln detested this man, I know. The idea that Mr. Lincoln would go to Tom Lewis and reveal to him his religious convictions, is to me, and to all who know Mr. Lincoln and Tom Lewis, too absurd.

The introduction of this Lewis as a witness demonstrates the paucity of evidence to be obtained this side of the question among Lincoln's neighbors. Reed, living in a city of twenty thousand inhabitants, many of them the personal friends of Abraham Lincoln, after a vigorous search for evidence, is able only to present this pitiable apology.

I have reason to believe that the letters of Edwards and Lewis were drafted, not by the persons whose signatures they bear, but by the Rev. J. A. Reed.

We come next to the testimony of Noah Brooks. Mr. Edwards, supported by Mr. Lewis, states that Lincoln was converted soon after Dr. Smith located at Springfield, and about the time of his son Eddie's death. Dr. Smith came to Springfield in 1848, and Eddie died toward the close of the same year. Dr. Smith, in his letter, does not state when Lincoln's conversion took place, but it is understood from other sources that he claimed that it occurred about the year 1858. Mr. Brooks, in his letter to Dr. Reed, says: "Speaking to me of the change which had come upon him, he said, while he could not fix any definite time, yet it was after he came here [Washington], and I am very positive that in his own mind he identified it with about the time of Willie's death."

Willie's death occurred in February, 1862, nearly fourteen years after the death of Eddie, and four years after Smith claimed to have converted Lincoln. Thus it will be seen that these witnesses nullify each other. The testimony of each is contradicted and refuted by the testimony of the other two. Mr. Edwards says that Lincoln was converted in 1848. This is contradicted by the testimony of both Smith and Brooks. According to Dr. Smith his conversion happened about 1858. This is contradicted by the testimony of both Edwards and Brooks. Mr. Brooks is quite positive that it took place about the time of Willie's death, in 1862. This, in turn, is contradicted by the testimony of both Edwards and Smith. If Mr. Edwards is right, both Dr. Smith and Mr. Brooks are wrong. If Dr. Smith is correct, both Mr. Edwards and Mr. Brooks are incorrect. If Mr. Brooks has stated the truth both Mr. Edwards and Dr. Smith have stated falsehoods.

The testimony of these witnesses does not strengthen Reed's case, but weakens it. The testimony of two of them is self-evidently false, and this is a sufficient reason for doubting the truthfulness of the third. Had the evidence of neither Edwards nor Smith been invalidated by the evidence of the others, the fact that Lincoln is so generally conceded to have been an unbeliever up to the time that he became President, would render it unworthy of consideration. The testimony of Brooks alone demands notice. Did Lincoln change his belief after he left Springfield and went to Washington? The evidence upon this point is decisive.

The man who stood nearest to President Lincoln at Washington – nearer than any clergyman or newspaper correspondent – was his private secretary, Col. John G. Nicolay. In a letter dated May 27, 1865, Colonel Nicolay says: "Mr. Lincoln did not, to my knowledge, in any way change his religious ideas, opinions, or beliefs from the time, he left Springfield to the day of his death."

In a letter to his old friend, Judge Wakefield, written after Willie's death, he declared that his earlier views of the unsoundness of the Christian scheme of salvation, and the human origin of the Scriptures, had become clearer and stronger with advancing years, and he did not think he should ever change them.

After his assassination Mrs. Lincoln said: "Mr. Lincoln had no hope and no faith in the usual acceptance of these words." His lifelong, friend and executor, Judge David Davis, affirmed the same: "He had no faith in the Christian sense of the term." His biographer, Colonel Lamon, intimately acquainted with him in Illinois, and with him during all the years that he lived in Washington, says: "Never in all that time did he let fall from his lips or his pen an expression which remotely implied the slightest faith in Jesus as the son of God and the Savior of men."

Why do the statements of these witnesses, Smith, Edwards, and Brooks, not agree respecting the date of Lincoln's conversion? When their testimony was given, Smith was in Scotland, Edwards was in Illinois, and Brooks was in New York.

If he was converted, why was the fact not revealed before his death? Why did these men wait until he died to make these statements to the world? Simply because the dead can make no reply.

Had Lincoln been converted, the news would have been wafted on the wings of lightning from one end of the continent to the other. It would have been published in every newspaper; it would have been proclaimed from every pulpit; it would have been a topic of conversation at every fireside. When Henry Wilson, a man of far less note than Lincoln, was converted to Christianity, the fact was heralded all over the land.

Lincoln's home was twice visited by death during his lifetime, and both occasions have been seized upon to assert that he experienced a change of heart. The death of a beloved child is no common sorrow, and the womanly tenderness of Lincoln's heart made it doubly poignant to him. "When death entered his household," says his friend, George W. Julian, "his sorrow was so consuming that it could only be measured by the singular depth and intensity of his love." That Mr. Edwards and Mr. Brooks did each observe a change in the demeanor of the grief-stricken father, following the sad events referred to, is not improbable. But a manifestation of sorrow is no proof of a theological change.

Three of Reed's witnesses remain – three clergymen – Dr. Sunderland, Dr. Miner, and Dr. Gurley. Dr. Sunderland is a man of distinction. He has had the honor of praying for the United States Senate and officiating at the marriage of a President. Yet, distinction is not always the badge of honesty. W. H. Burr, a literary gentleman, of Washington, writing to a Boston paper in 1880, paid the following tribute to Dr. Sunderland's veracity: "He can probably put more falsehood and calumny in a page of foolscap than any priest out of prison."

Mr. Sunderland called upon the President in 1862. In his letter to Reed he says: "For one half hour [he] poured forth a volume of the deepest Christian philosophy I ever heard." Notwithstanding ten years had elapsed since that visit, he proceeded to give from memory a verbatim report of Lincoln's remarks. The report is too long to reproduce in this work, and even if correct, would add but little to the weight of Christian evidence already presented. It is merely an ethical discourse, and aside from a few indirect admissions in favor of Christianity for which Sunderland doubtless drew upon his imagination, there is nothing that Paine or any other Deist might not with propriety have uttered. Those who wish to peruse Mr. Sunderland's letter will find it in *Scribner's Monthly* for July, 1873.

Dr. Miner, like Dr. Sunderland, had a quiet chat with the President, and what was said he assures us is too deeply engraved on his memory ever to be effaced. But, unlike Dr. Sunderland, he does not favor us with a transcript of it. He does not repeat a word that was uttered. He states, however, that, "If Mr. Lincoln was not really an experimental Christian, he was acting like one." But how does an experimental Christian act? If he behaves himself, if he is intelligent and honest, his actions are not materially different from those of a good Freethinker. Dr. Miner did not believe that Lincoln was an experimental Christian, and in his article there is an implied admission that he knew nothing about his religion.

He says that, "Like the immortal Washington, he believed in the efficacy of prayer." The comparison is happily drawn. Lincoln probably did believe as much in the efficacy of prayer as Washington; that is to say, he did not believe in it at all, in the evangelical sense. There is no evidence that Washington believed in prayer, no proof that he ever uttered a prayer. That story about his praying at Valley Forge is as truly a myth as the story about the hatchet. The Rev. E. D. Neill, an eminent Episcopal minister, and a relative of the person who is reported to have seen Washington engaged in prayer, pronounces it a fiction.

Dr. Gurley is represented as saying: "I considered him sound not only on the truth of the Christian religion, but on all its fundamental doctrines and teachings." This, remember, is from a Calvinistic standpoint. Lincoln, then, not only accepted Christianity, but its most ultra variety Calvinism. He believed in original sin, predestination (including infant damnation), particular redemption, irresistible grace, and perseverance of the saints. Because he sometimes went with his wife to the Presbyterian church, of which she was an adherent, the priests of this denomination have the contemptible assurance to assert that he was a rigid Calvinist!

When he died, Dr. Gurley, being Mrs. Lincoln's pastor, delivered the funeral oration in Washington. In that oration Dr. Gurley did not affirm that Lincoln was a Christian, a thing he would not have failed to do had it been true. Long after Lincoln's death, Dr. Gurley, if Reed has correctly reported him, makes a statement that he had not the courage to make over his dead body.

A reputable Christian gentleman, of Springfield, who desires to have his name withheld from, the public, declares that Dr. Gurley knew and admitted that Lincoln was a disbeliever in Christianity.

It is quite probable that Gurley did not state in full what Reed reports him to have stated. A man who can take up his pen and at one sitting indite a score of falsehoods and misrepresentations, as Reed, on a subsequent occasion, is shown to have done, cannot be relied upon for accuracy as a reporter.

The reader has doubtless not failed to notice the introduction of a claim by Reed to the effect that Lincoln at the time of his assassination was intending to unite with the church. That the idea was suggested by Reed is shown by the fact that no less than three of these witnesses, including Reed, allude to it. Reed says: "While it is to be regretted that Mr. Lincoln was not spared to indicate his religious sentiments by a profession of his faith in accordance with the institutions of the Christian religion, yet is very clear that he had this step in view." Dr. Gurley is made to say: "It was his intention soon to make a profession of religion." Mr. Brooks says: "I absorbed [the porosity of some of these witnesses is remarkable] the firm conviction that Mr. Lincoln . . . was seriously considering the step which would formally connect him with the visible church on earth."

This *dernier resort* of an argument has been repeated respecting nearly every notable person who has died outside of the church. Soon after the publication of Reed's lecture, the *New York World* contained the following pertinent answer to this stale fabrication:

> It is admitted by Mr. Reed and everybody else that Mr. Lincoln was a working Infidel up to a very late period of his life, that he wrote a book and labored earnestly to make prose-lytes to his own views, that he never publicly recanted, and that he never joined the church. Upon those who, in the face of these tremendous facts, allege that he was nevertheless a Christian lies the burden of proof. Let them produce it or forever hold their peace. In the mean time it is a sad and puerile subterfuge to argue that he *would* have been a Christian if he had lived long enough, and to lament that he was not 'spared' for that purpose. He *had* been spared fifty-six years and surrounded by every circumstance that might soften his heart and every influence that might elevate his faith. If he was at that late, that fatal hour standing thus gloomily without the pale, what reason have we to suppose that he intended ever to enter?

Reed speaks of "the poverty of his early religious instruction," apparently forgetting that he was raised by Christian parents. His father was a church-member, his mother was a church-member, and his stepmother was a church-member. Reed states, also, that the books he read were all of an anti-religious character. Holland, on the contrary, declares that better books than those he read could not have been chosen from the richest library. The fact is, Abraham Lincoln did not become an Infidel to Christianity from a lack of knowledge respecting its claims. He thoroughly examined its claims, and rejected them because he found them untenable.

One important feature of this subject Reed has either inadvertently omitted or purposely ignored, and that is in regard to the validity of the Bateman story. As the result of previous controversy this evidence had been rendered valueless. Lincoln's partner had declared it to be false, had asserted that Mr. Bateman in private conversations acknowledged it to be in part untrue, and announced his readiness to substantiate his assertions if Mr. Bateman could be prevailed upon to permit the publication of his notes of these conversations taken at the time. If Mr. Herndon's affirmations were true, it destroyed the testimony of Holland and Bateman; if untrue, it challenged Mr. Bateman to reaffirm the statements recorded by Holland, and allow the seal of privacy to be removed from his conversations on the subject. Why did Mr. Reed not rehabilitate this damaged evidence? Did he forget it? No, it is plainly evident that he did not dare to attempt it.

In reviewing this Calvinistic *coterie* of witnesses (they are all Calvinists, and nearly all Presbyterians), one is struck with the formidable display of theological appendages. What an imposing array of D.D.'s! Rev. J. A. Reed, D.D.! Rev. James Smith, D.D.! Rev. Byron Sunderland, D.D.! Rev. Mr. Miner, D.D.! Rev. Mr. Gurley, D.D.! It was a desperate case – divinity was sick and needed doctoring. The doctors of divinity were accordingly called in, and prescribed "The Later Life and Religious Sentiments of Abraham Lincoln," after which it was supposed that divinity would recover. He may be better, but it is painfully apparent that some of these D.D.'s are themselves sadly in need of doctor.

CHAPTER FOUR:
Review of Christian Testimony –
Arnold and Other Witnesses

☆　☆　☆　☆

Arnold's *Life of Lincoln* – Claims Concerning Lincoln's Religious
Belief – Address to Negroes of Baltimore – Carpenter Hawley
Willets – Pious Nurse – *Western Christian Advocate*
Illinois Clergyman – Barrows – Vinton – Simpson

With the Christian masses, whose minds have become warped by the bigoted teachings of their clerical leaders, nothing affects the reputation of a man so much as his religious belief. Public men who are disbelievers are fully cognizant of this, and generally refrain from expressing sentiments that would tend to alienate those upon whom the retention of their positions depends. Biographers understand this, too, and are likewise aware that a dead Infidel is as cordially hated as a live one. They know that a cold reception awaits their works unless they are able to clothe the characters of their subjects in the robes of popular superstition. Mr. Arnold realized this when he wrote his *Life of Lincoln*. He had been most forcibly reminded of the fact by the fate of two biographies of his own subject which had already appeared in Holland's and Lamon's. Holland's work by catering to popular prejudice, regardless of truth, had been financially a success; Lamon's work, by adhering to truth, regardless of popular prejudice, had been financially a failure.

Determined to profit by these examples, and intimidated by the threats and entreaties of those who had resolved to secure for Christianity the influence of the Great Emancipator's name,

Arnold dared not give the facts regarding Lincoln's religious belief. Nor is it to be presumed that he desired to. He had previously appeared as a special pleader for the popular faith.

He affirms that, "No more reverent Christian than Lincoln ever sat in the Executive chair, not excepting Washington." The fact is, when Arnold wrote his biography of Lincoln, no very reverent Christian ever had occupied the Executive chair. Previous to the installation of Gen. B. H. Harrison no real orthodox Christian communicant had held the office of President.

If Mr. Arnold knew no more about Lincoln's religion than he appears to have known about Washington's, a more charitable reason than those suggested might be assigned for his statements concerning the former. Washington, like Lincoln, has been claimed by the church; yet, Washington, like Lincoln, was a Deist. This is admitted even by the leading churchmen of his day. Three of the most eminent divines of his age, and the three to whom he was most intimately related in a social way, were Bishop White, Rev. Dr. Abercrombie, and Rev. Dr. Ashbel Green. Bishop White declares that Washington was not a communicant, as claimed by some, and intimates that he was a disbeliever. The Rev. Dr. Abercrombie, whose church he attended while he was President, said: "Washington was a Deist." The Rev. Dr. Ashbel Green, chaplain to Congress during his administration, said: "Like nearly all the founders of the Republic, he was not a Christian, but a Deist."

Arnold presents the following as the basis of Lincoln's religion, and proofs of his Christianity: "(1) Belief in the existence of God, (2) in the immortality of the soul, (3) in the Bible as the revelation of God to man, (4) in the efficacy and duty of prayer, (5) in reverence toward the Almighty, and (6) in love and charity to man."

1. Belief in the existence of God." This does not prove a belief in Christianity. The Jew believes in the existence of God; the Mohammedan believes in the existence of God; the Deistic Infidel believes in the existence of God.

2. "Belief in the immortality of the soul." That he believed in the immortality of the soul is a claim that cannot be

clearly established; and even if it could, would not confirm the assumption that he was a Christian. Deists, many of them, believe in the doctrine of immortality. Paine believed in immortality; Voltaire believed in immortality.

3. "Belief in the Bible as the revelation of God to man." This, if true, would be evidence of his Christianity; but, unfortunately for Mr. Arnold's claim, Lincoln did not entertain this belief.

4. "Belief in the efficacy and duty of prayer." This, in the orthodox sense of these terms, is not true; and if it were, would not furnish conclusive evidence that he was a Christian. Jews pray; Mohammedans pray; Buddhists pray; some Deists pray. Franklin believed in the efficacy and duty of prayer, and Franklin was an Infidel.

5. "Belief in reverence to the Almighty." This does not demonstrate a belief in Christianity, for all Deists believe in reverence to the Almighty.

6. "Belief in love and charity to man." When it can be shown that only Christians believe in love and charity, then will it be time to affirm that Lincoln was a Christian.

Arnold confounds Christianity with Deism. In the following words he admits that Lincoln was simply a Deist: "Not orthodox, not a man of creeds; he was a man of simple trust in God." When the subject of Lincoln's belief was once mentioned to Mr. Arnold, he said: "Lincoln was a rational Christian because he believed in morality." With equal propriety one might say of an upright Christian, "He is a rational Freethinker because he believes in morality."

"His reply to the Negroes of Baltimore," he says, "ought to silence forever those who charge him with unbelief." This alleged reply of Lincoln was as follows:

> In regard to the Great Book I have only to say that it is the best gift which God has given to man. All the good from the Savior of the world is communicated to us through this book. But for this book we could not know right from wrong. All those things

desirable to man are contained in it.[1]

The writer of this was in Washington when the colored deputation from Baltimore presented the President with a $500 Bible. The papers mentioned the fact at the time, but no such speech as Lincoln is said to have made appeared in the reports. About two months later, this apocryphal version of his remarks on the occasion referred to, made its appearance.

The first two sentences contained in this speech (the only part of it that Arnold has quoted), Lincoln, if a Christian, might have uttered. They are words that any intelligent Christian might, from his standpoint, with propriety affirm. We are familiar with these claims. We are also familiar with the claim embodied in the last two sentences. They are repeatedly made. But they are made only by very ignorant persons, or by clerical hypocrites who try to impose upon the ignorance and credulity of their hearers. Had Lincoln been a Christian he would not have used these words, because he was too intelligent to believe them, and too honest to pretend to believe them.

Concerning this speech, Lincoln's partner, Mr. Herndon, thus vigorously, yet truthfully, remarks:

> I am aware of the fraud committed on Mr. Lincoln in reporting some insane remarks supposed to have been made by him, in 1864, on the presentation of a Bible to him by the colored people of Baltimore. No sane man ever uttered such folly, and no sane man will ever believe it. In that speech Mr. Lincoln is made to say: "But for this book we could not know right from wrong." Does any human being believe that Lincoln ever uttered this? What did the whole race of man do to know right from wrong during the countless years that passed before this book was given to the world? How did the struggling race of man build up its grand civilizations in the world before this book was given to mankind? What do the millions of people now living, who never heard of this book, do to know how to distinguish right from wrong? Was Lincoln a fool, an ass, a hypocrite, or a combination of them all?

---

1. *Lincoln Memorial Album*, p. 340.

or is this speech – this supposed – this fraudulent speech – a lie?

Arnold would have his readers believe that this speech is genuine. And yet it is plainly evident that he himself does not believe it. He mutilates it by omitting the more orthodox portion of it – the very portion he would have retained had he believed it to be genuine. The first part would suffice to serve his purpose; the remainder he knew was too incredible for belief and would stamp the whole as a fraud.

Arnold says: "The veil between him and the supernatural was very thin." Yes, so thin that he easily saw through it and recognized the greater part of it to be a sham.

"His faith in a Divine Providence began at his mother's knee, and ran through all the changes of his life." I do not desire to charge Mr. Arnold with plagiarism, but the foregoing recalls the following much admired passage to be found in Holland: "This unwavering faith in a Divine Providence began at his mother's knee, and ran like a thread of gold through all the inner experiences of his life."[2]

There is much in Arnold's biography, aside from the above, to suggest that Holland's work formed the basis and model of his own. While more accurate in the main than Holland's *Life*, Arnold's *Life* is in some respects equally unreliable, and less readable.

Adverting to the many fraudulent stories that have been circulated concerning Lincoln, in an address delivered in London, Mr. Arnold said: "The newspapers in America have always been full of Lincoln stories and anecdotes, some true and many fabulous." Unfortunately for the cause of truth, Mr. Arnold has himself recorded some of these fabulous stories, not because he deemed them authentic, but because they agreed with his preconceived prejudices, or the prejudices of those whom he wished to please.

Mr. Carpenter says: "I would scarcely have called Mr. Lincoln a religious man, and yet I believe him to have been a sincere

---

2. *Life of Lincoln*, pp. 61, 62

Christian."

In a letter, Mr. Herndon makes the following correction in regard to his friend Carpenter's statement:

> Mr. Carpenter has not expressed his own ideas correctly. To say that a man is a Christian and yet not a religious man is absurd. *Religion* is the generic term. including all forms of religion; *Christianity* is a specific term representing one form of religion. Carpenter means to say that Mr. Lincoln was a religious man but not a Christian, and this is the truth.

It is unfortunate that while in many cases we have several words to express the same idea, the same word in many cases is employed to express different ideas. Ideas thus become confused. If the terms *morality, religion,* and *Christianity,* were always used in their legitimate sense – used to express the ideas of which they were the original signs – much trouble and ambiguity would be avoided. As it is, they are promiscuously used as interchangeable terms. Many use the word *religion* and even *Christianity* when they mean *morality.* Mr. Carpenter uses the word *religious* in its proper sense, and the word *Christian* to mean a *moral man.* The following examples will serve to illustrate the various forms employed to express the thought now under consideration:

"I would scarcely have called Mr. Lincoln a religious man, and yet I believe him to have been a sincere Christian." – *Carpenter.*

"I would scarcely have called Mr. Lincoln a Christian, and yet I believe him to have been a truly *religious man.*" – *Herndon.*

I would scarcely have called Mr. Lincoln a religious man, and yet I believe him to have been a truly moral man. – *Author.*

We all desire to express substantially the same thought. I do not wish to dictate to Mr. Carpenter and Mr. Herndon what words they shall employ to convey an idea, but this explanation is essential to a proper understanding of the question in dispute and will help to reconcile much of the apparently conflicting testimony presented in this work.

As Lincoln was in a certain sense a Deist, the religious element was not entirely wanting in him, and hence the statement of Mr. Herndon that he was a religious man is, in a degree, true. The basis of Carpenter's work was a series of articles contributed to the New York *Independent.* When it was decided to publish these in book form, to swell them into a volume of the desired size, to his personal reminiscences he added many of the stories pertaining to Lincoln then going the rounds of the press. Although he was as it were a member of Lincoln's household six months he failed to hear from Lincoln's lips a word expressing a belief in Christianity. These apocryphal stories, and these alone, contain all the evidences of Lincoln's alleged piety to be found in Carpenter's book. And his admission that Lincoln was not a religious man disproves them.

Mr. Hawley professed to believe that Lincoln was a Christian, but he had no personal knowledge of the fact, although his neighbor for many years. The only reasons he was able to adduce upon which to predicate his belief were the Bateman story and his farewell speech on leaving Springfield. The former has been exploded; the latter proves nothing.

During all the later years of his life Lincoln generally refrained from expressing his anti-Christian opinions, except to friends who shared his views. This silence, in connection with his sterling moral character, might lead some of his Christian neighbors to suppose that he was a believer, the more especially as Christians are generally ignorant of the extent of unbelief, and are loath to believe that a person, unless he openly avows his disbelief, can be an Infidel.

According to Mr. Willets, Lincoln, during the war, had an attack of what he thought might be a "change of heart." He consulted a pious lady in regard to it and requested her to describe to him the symptoms attending this theological disease. She defined "a true religious experience" as "a conviction of one's own sinfulness and weakness, and personal need of the Savior for strength and support." She said that "when one was really brought to feel his need of divine help, and to seek the aid of the Holy Spirit for strength and guidance, it was satisfactory evidence of his having been born again." Lincoln replied that if what she had told him was "a correct view of this great subject," he hoped he was a Christian. But was this a correct view of it? I was not aware that conviction constituted conversion. We have been taught that conviction is but a preliminary step toward conversion. If Lincoln relied upon this as a true exposition of this doctrine, the genuineness of his conversion may well be questioned.

It is to be regretted that Mr. Willets did not give the name of his informant. As it is, we do not know whether to credit "a lady acquaintance of his," or himself, with the invention of a first-class fiction.

In regard to the story of the "Pious Nurse," we have not even a clergyman to vouch for its authenticity. We do not know the name of this witness; we do not know whom she communicated the story to; we do not know when nor where it made its first appearance. We only know that for years it has been floating through the columns of the religious press, a companion-piece to Washington's devotional exercise at Valley Forge.

"History," said Napoleon," is a set of lies agreed upon." Of the many lies agreed upon by Christian writers in making up the history of Lincoln, none has become more thoroughly established than the one originally published by the *Western Christian Advocate*. It has been incorporated into the works of a score of historians and biographers, and is almost universally accepted as a historical fact.

Nearly all the pious stories relating to Lincoln, while palpably false in the eyes of those who knew him, are yet of such a nature as to render a complete refutation of them extremely difficult. The story under consideration, however, is of a different character. Its truthfulness or falsity could at the time of its publication have been easily ascertained. If true, any member of Lincoln's cabinet could have verified it. I knew that it was untrue – at least I knew that a Cabinet meeting had never been transformed into a prayer meeting at Lincoln's suggestion. I finally resolved to demonstrate its falsity if possible. But a quarter of a century had passed away, and every member of Lincoln's Cabinet was dead save one – Hugh McCulloch, his last Secretary of the Treasury. With the aid of a friend, Mr. N. P. Stockbridge, of Ft. Wayne, Ind., an old acquaintance of Mr. McCulloch's, I succeeded in bringing the matter before this only surviving witness, and received from his pen, in February, 1891, the following prompt denial:

> The description of what occurred at the Executive Mansion, when the intelligence was received of the surrender of the Confederate forces, which you quote from the *Western Christian Advocate,* is not only absolutely groundless, but absurd. After I became Secretary of the Treasury I was present at every Cabinet meeting, and I never saw Mr. Lincoln or any of his ministers upon his knees or in tears.
>
> We were not especially jubilant over Lee's surrender, for this we had been prepared for some days. The time for our great rejoicing was a little earlier. After Sherman had commenced his celebrated march to the sea, and long and weary days had passed without any reliable reports from him, we were filled with anxiety and apprehension. It was when the news came that he and his army, in excellent condition, were in the neighborhood of Charleston, that our joy was irrepressible; not only because of their safety, but because it was an assurance that the days of the Confederacy were nearly ended. With Grant before Richmond in command of superior forces, and Sherman with the finest army in the world, ready to move northward, everybody felt that the war must be soon concluded, and that the Union was safe.
>
> We were, of course, happy when General Lee and his severely tried soldiers laid down their arms, but this, as I have said, was not unexpected. It was when our anxiety in regard to Sherman was succeeded by hopefulness and confidence that our joy became exuberant. But there was no such exhibition of it as has been published by the *Advocate.*

An "Illinois Clergyman" reports Lincoln as saying that when he left Springfield he was not a Christian, that when his son Willie died he was not a Christian, but that when he visited the battlefield of Gettysburg he gave his heart to Christ. Christians cite the testimony of this anonymous witness, seemingly unconscious of the fact that if true it refutes the testimony of every other Christian witness. If this statement be true what becomes of the testimony of Holland and Bateman? What becomes of the testimony of Reed's witnesses? The testimony of Brooks invalidated the testimony of every other witness; the testimony of this Illinois clergyman invalidates the testimony of Brooks itself.

Reed did not present this evidence, doubtless aware that his lecture already contained a sufficient number of discrepancies. He was thoughtful enough, however, to anticipate it. He had Dr. Gurley refer to Lincoln's conversion as taking place "after the death of his son Willie and his visit to the battlefield of Gettysburg." These events are referred to as if they occurred in close proximity to each other; whereas the death of Willie occurred during the first year of his administration, his visit to Gettysburg less than seventeen months before his assassination.

The passage quoted from Dr. Barrows contains six specific affirmations.

1. "In the anxious uncertainties of the great war, he gradually rose to the heights where Jehovah became to him the sublimest of realities, the ruler of nations."

Collect all the utterances of Abraham Lincoln, all the letters he ever wrote, all the speeches he ever delivered, all the state papers he gave to the public; and from this full store of words that fell from his lips and flowed from his pen, I challenge Dr. Barrows to produce one word expressing a recognition of Jehovah. Jehovah was to him, not the sublimest of realities," not "the ruler of nations," but a hideous phantom. He recognized a God, but his God was not Jehovah, the God of Dr. Barrows.

2. "When he wrote his immortal Proclamation, he invoked upon it not only 'the considerate judgment of mankind,' but 'the gracious favor of Almighty God.'"

When he wrote his immortal Proclamation he did not invoke "the gracious favor of Almighty God." This instrument, as drafted by Lincoln, contained no allusion to God. The paragraph containing the words quoted was drafted by Secretary Chase and inserted in the Proclamation at his urgent request after it was printed and ready for delivery.

3. "When darkness gathered over the brave armies fighting for the nation's life, this strong man, in the early morning, knelt and wrestled in prayer with him who holds in his hand the fate of empires."

A "Christian lady from Massachusetts" (name unknown), and a Christian gentleman from New York (Noah Brooks), declare that Lincoln was accustomed to pray. This declaration is echoed by Arnold, and reëchoed by Barrows. If true, is it not strange that a hospital nurse and a newspaper reporter were in possession of the fact while his most intimate friends were entirely ignorant of it?

4. "When the clouds lifted above the carnage of Gettysburg, he gave his heart to the Lord Jesus Christ."

This is the fifth time that Lincoln gave his heart to Christ. The above statement is the vital one in Dr. Barrows's testimony – the keystone in the arch comprising "the religious aspects" of Lincoln's Presidential career. The others, even if true, only prove a Theistic belief. This statement affirms that he became a Christian – a statement evidently based upon the anonymous story of the "Illinois clergyman." Between the original presented by the "Illinois clergyman" at large, and that presented by the Illinois clergyman from Chicago, however, a grave discrepancy appears. From the time that "the clouds lifted above the carnage of Gettysburg" to the time that Lincoln visited its cemetery, a period of twenty weeks had elapsed. Now, did Lincoln give his heart to Christ when the battle ended on the 3rd of July, as stated by the one, or not until he stood upon the battle-field on the 19th of November, as asserted by the other? This is a question that we leave for the Illinois clergymen themselves to decide.

5. "When he pronounced his matchless oration on the chief battle-field of the war, he gave expression to the resolve that 'this nation, under God, should have a new birth of freedom.'"

This simple Deistic phrase, "under God," is the only utterance of a religious character to be found in that oration. When this speech was delivered, Lincoln, it is claimed, had experienced a change of heart and consecrated himself to Christ. This address furnishes an overwhelming refutation of the claim. At the dedication of a cemetery, surrounded by thousands of graves, he ignores Christianity, and even the doctrine of immortality.

6. "And when he wrote his last Inaugural Address, he gave to it the lofty tone of an old Hebrew psalm."

This is true; and it is likewise true that in that document he made no more reference to Christianity than did the Hebrew psalmist who lived and wrote a thousand years before it had its birth.

The *Lincoln Memorial Album*, in which Dr. Barrows's article appears, contains the offerings of two hundred contributors, twenty of them divines, and among them Lyman Abbot, Dr. Bellows, Theodore L. Cuyler, Robert Collyer, Bishop Coxe, Dr. Crosby, Bishop Haven, Philip Schaaf, and Bishop Simpson. The work is prefaced with a biographical sketch of Lincoln, written by Isaac N. Arnold, in which he makes substantially the same statements regarding Lincoln's belief as those made in his *Life of Lincoln*. Aside from this, Dr. Barrows is the only one of these two hundred memorialists who ventures to affirm that Lincoln was a Christian.

The story of Dr. Vinton, too absurd to demand serious consideration – apparently too incredible for belief – is yet believed by thousands. When such fabulous tales are told by men who are looked upon as the exponents of morality, and published in papers and periodicals that are presumed to be the repositories only of truth, it is not strange that such stories as Washington's Praying at Valley Forge, Ethan Allen and His Daughter, Don't Unchain the Tiger, Paine's Recanting, and a thousand and one other pious fictions of a similar character, have gained popular credence. To read the fabrications of this class pertaining to Lincoln alone, one would suppose that this astute statesman, this Chief Magistrate of a great nation, this Commander-in-Chief of two millions of soldiers, engaged in the most stupendous civil conflict the world has known, occupied the greater portion of his time in studying the Scriptures, poring over doctrinal sermons, participating in prayer-meetings led by pious nurses, and weeping upon the necks of clerical visitors.

Bishop Simpson's remarks have been presented, not because they furnish any proofs of Lincoln's reputed Christianity, but because he was one of the clergymen who officiated at Lincoln's funeral, and because his words on that occasion have been cited in support of this claim. But he does not assert that Lincoln was a Christian. He simply testifies to his belief and trust in God – to his Deistic faith – nothing more.

I am aware that in some of the published reports of his address there have been interpolated words intended to convey the idea that Lincoln accepted Christ. Bishop Simpson, I am sure, never authorized the insertion of these words. They express a claim he never made – a claim he certainly did not make on the day of Lincoln's interment.

In his funeral address at Washington, Dr. Gurley did not affirm that Lincoln was a Christian, or that he was intending to make a profession of religion. Bishop Simpson, in his oration at Springfield, made no mention of these claims, and Dr. Gurley and Bishop Simpson are known to have held a consultation before that oration was delivered.

This silence is conclusive evidence that these men knew that Lincoln was an unbeliever. Commenting on this notable omission, Mr. Herndon says:

> Bishop Simpson delivered the funeral oration, and in that oration there was not one word about Mr. Lincoln's Christianity. Bishop Simpson was Lincoln's friend; Dr. Gurley was Lincoln's pastor in Washington. Now these men knew, or had reason to know, Lincoln's religion, and the world would have heard of his Christianity on the day of his burial if it had been known. But Simpson and Gurley are silent – dumb before the Christian world.

One of the most beautiful and exhaustive tributes ever paid to Lincoln, aside from the matchless tribute paid by Colonel Ingersoll, is that from the pen of Bishop Simpson which appears in the *Lincoln Memorial Album*. In this tribute he does not make even the remotest allusion to Lincoln's religious belief. He appears to have heeded the advice tendered by a less discreet Christian writer, and recognized the fact that, from his standpoint, the less said about the subject the better. Had all Christians acted as wisely and as honorably in this matter as Bishop Simpson, this controversy about Lincoln's religion would never have arisen.

I have now reviewed the testimony of these witnesses. Tested in the crucible of honest criticism, little remains of their statements save the dross of falsehood and error. I may be charged with unjust severity toward these witnesses, nearly all of whom are men of recognized respectability and distinction. But a majority of them have testified to what they know to be false, and against those who knowingly bear false witness no censure can be too severe. Thousands of Christian men and women, misled by this false testimony, honestly believe and contend that Lincoln was a Christian. Against these I have not an unkind word to offer. But I am resolved to disabuse their minds of this erroneous belief. Painful as the birth of an unwelcome idea is, they shall know the truth.

CHAPTER FIVE:
Testimony of Hon. William H. Herndon –
Published Testimony
☆ ☆ ☆ ☆

Herndon's Association with Lincoln – Character – Writings
Competency as a Witness – The Abbott Letter – Contribution
to the *Liberal Age* – Article in the *Truth Seeker* – Herndon's
Life of Lincoln

Having presented and reviewed the evidence in behalf of
the affirmative of this question, the evidence in support of the
negative will next be given, and in consideration of his long and
intimate association with Lincoln, and the character and compre-
hensiveness of his testimony, the first to testify will be Hon.
Wm. H. Herndon, of Springfield, Ill.

In 1843, Lincoln formed a partnership with Mr. Herndon
in the law business, which existed for a period of twenty-two
years, and was only dissolved by the bullet of the assassin. The
strong attachment that these men had for each other is illustrated
in the following touching incident, related in *The Everyday Life
of Lincoln*:

> When he was about to leave for Washington, he went
> to the dingy little law office which had sheltered his saddest hours.
> He sat down on the couch and said to his law-partner, Herndon,
> "Billy, you and I have been together more than twenty years, and
> have never 'passed a word.' Will you let my name stay on the
> old sign till I come back from Washington?" The tears started
> to Mr. Herndon's eyes. He put out his hand. "Mr. Lincoln," said
> he, "I will never have any other partner while you live;" and to

the day of the assassination all the doings of the firm were in the name of "Lincoln & Herndon."[1]

Mr. Herndon died in 1891. Though younger than his illustrious partner, he was at the time of his death well advanced in years. He had retired from the active practice of law, and resided at his country home near Springfield. He was noted for his rugged honesty, for his broad philanthropy, and for his strong and original mental qualities. He was one of the pioneers in the antislavery movement, and one of the founders of the Republican party. He was the Republican nominee for Presidential Elector of the Springfield district when the first Republican ticket, Fremont and Dayton, was placed in the field. Governor Bissell, Governor Yates and Governor Oglesby successively appointed him Bank Commissioner of Illinois. His talents were recognized and his friendship was sought by many of the most eminent men in the nation. Garrison stopped for weeks at his home; Theodore Parker was his guest; Horace Greeley was his devoted friend, and Charles Sumner was his friend and correspondent.

When Lincoln and Herndon were first thrown into each other's society, Lincoln's mind was dwelling, for the most part, in the theological (or rather anti-theological) world, while Herndon's found a most congenial habitation in the world of politics. They were destined to exercise an important influence in molding each other's characters. Herndon was indebted chiefly to Lincoln for the religious views he entertained, while Lincoln was indebted mainly to Herndon for the political principles which he finally espoused. Colonel Lamon, in his *Life of Lincoln*, gives the following truthful sketch of the character of the man whom Lincoln made a Deist, and who in turn made an Abolitionist of Lincoln. Alluding to the Abolitionists of Illinois, as they appeared in 1854, when Lincoln took his stand on the side of freedom, Lamon says:

Chief among them was Owen Lovejoy; and second to

---

1. *Everyday Life of Lincoln*, p. 377.

him, if second to any, was William H. Herndon. But the position of this latter gentleman was one of singular embarrassment. According to himself, he was an Abolitionist "some time before he was born," and hitherto he had made his "calling and election sure" by every word and act of a life devoted to political philanthropy and disinterested political labors. While the two great national parties divided the suffrages of the people, North and South, everything in his eyes was dead. He detested the bargains by which those parties were in the habit of composing sectional troubles, and sacrificing the principle of freedom. When the Whig party paid its breath to time, he looked upon its last agonies as but another instance of divine retribution. He had no patience with time-servers, and regarded with indignant contempt the policy which would postpone the natural rights of an enslaved race to the success of parties and politicians. He stood by at the sacrifice of the Whig party in Illinois with the spirit of Paul when he held the clothes of them that stoned Stephen. He believed it was for the best, and hoped to see a new party rise in its place, great in the fervor of its faith, and animated by the spirit of Wilberforce, Garrison, and the Lovejoys. He was a fierce zealot, and gloried proudly in his title of "fanatic;" for it was his conviction that fanatics were at all times the salt of the earth, with power to save it from the blight that follows the wickedness of men. He believed in a God, but it was the God of Nature – the God of Socrates and Plato, as well as the God of Jacob. He believed in a Bible, but it was the open scroll of the universe; and in a religion clear and well defined, but it was a religion that scorned what he deemed the narrow slavery of verbal inspiration. Hot-blooded, impulsive, brave, morally and physically, careless of consequences when moved by a sense of individual duty, he was the very man to receive into his inmost heart the precepts of Mr. Seward's "higher law."[2]

His literary abilities, both as a speaker and as a writer, were of a high order. He had written a meritorious work on Mental Philosophy, and a *Life of Lincoln*, which had just been published when he died. In addition to numerous addresses upon historical,

---

2. *Life of Lincoln*, pp. 350, 351.

economical, and other subjects, he prepared and delivered several able and interesting lectures on Lincoln: "Abraham Lincoln and Ann Rutledge," a beautiful and touching representation of that pathetic and romantic love episode which forms one of the saddest chapters in Lincoln's history; "The Analysis of Lincoln's Character," which appears in the *Lincoln Memorial Album*, and "Lincoln's Religion," which was published in the *State Register,* of Springfield, Ill.

Carpenter, and in fact nearly every writer on Lincoln, has made free use of Herndon's writings. Carpenter declares that his "masterly 'Analysis of Lincoln's Character' has scarcely an equal in the annals of biographical literature." Both Holland and Lamon acknowledge that they were more deeply indebted to him in the preparation of their respective works than to any other person. The *Petersburg Democrat,* published in Menard county, where Lincoln spent the first years of his manhood, says: "Mr. Herndon was the law partner of Mr. Lincoln from 1843 to 1860, and knew his inner life better than any other man." The Sangamon county *Monitor,* of Springfield, where Lincoln lived for a quarter of a century, says: "Herndon knew Lincoln's views better than any man in America." Judge David Davis, the lifelong friend of Lincoln, in whose court both Lincoln and Herndon practiced for years, declared that Herndon knew more about Lincoln's religion than any other man.

In this chapter will be reproduced the evidence of Mr. Herndon that has already been made public.

The first elaborate exposition of Lincoln's Freethought views was made in 1870, in what is known as the "Abbott Letter," an article which Mr. Herndon by request contributed to the *Index,* a paper then published at Toledo, Ohio, and edited by Francis E. Abbott. The article was extensively copied and commented upon, and produced a profound sensation in the religious world, which, to a great extent, had been misled by such writers as Holland. The first and more important part of Mr. Herndon's article will now be presented:

Mr. ABBOTT: Some time since I promised you that I

would send a letter in relation to Mr. Lincoln's religion. I do so now. Before entering on that question, one or two preliminary remarks will help us to understand why he disagreed with the Christian world in its principles as well as in its theology. In the first place, Mr. Lincoln's mind was a purely logical mind; secondly, Mr. Lincoln was a purely practical man. He had no fancy or imagination, and not much emotion. He was a realist as opposed to an idealist. As a general rule, it is true that a purely logical mind has not much hope, if it ever has faith in the unseen and unknown. Mr. Lincoln had not much hope and no faith in things that lie outside of the domain of demonstration; he was so constituted, so organized, that he could believe nothing unless his senses or logic could reach it. I have often read to him a law point, a decision, or something I fancied. He could not understand it until he took the book out of my hand, and read the thing for himself. He was terribly, vexatiously skeptical. He could scarcely understand anything, unless he had time and place fixed in his mind.

I became acquainted with Mr. Lincoln in 1834, and I think I knew him well to the day of his death. His mind, when a boy in Kentucky, showed a certain gloom, an unsocial nature, a peculiar abstractedness, a bold and daring skepticism. In Indiana, from 1817 to 1830, it manifested the same qualities or attributes as in Kentucky: it only intensified, developed itself, along those lines in Indiana. He came to Illinois in 1830, and, after some little roving, settled in New Salem, now in Menard county and State of Illinois. This village lies about twenty miles northwest of this city. It was here that Mr. Lincoln became acquainted with a class of men the world never saw the like of before or since. They were large men – large in body and large in mind; hard to whip and never to be fooled. They were a bold, daring, and reckless sort of men; they were men of their own minds – believed what was demonstrable; were men of great common sense. With these men Mr. Lincoln was thrown; with them he lived, and with them he moved and almost had his being. They were skeptics all, scoffers some. These scoffers were good men, and their scoffs were protests against theology – loud protests against the follies of Christianity. They had never heard of Theism and the newer and better religious thoughts of this age. Hence, being natural skeptics, and being bold, brave men, they uttered their thoughts freely. They declared that Jesus was an illegitimate child. They were on, all occasions, when opportunity offered, debating the various questions of Christianity among themselves. They took their stand on common sense and on their own souls; and, though their arguments were rude and rough, no man could overthrow their homely logic. They riddled all divines, and not infrequently made them skeptics, disbelievers as bad as themselves. They were a jovial, healthful, generous, social, true, and manly set of people.

It was here and among these people that Mr. Lincoln was thrown. About the year 1834 he chanced to come across Volney's *Ruins* and some of Paine's theological works. He at once seized hold of them, and assimilated them into his own being. Volney and Paine became a part of Mr. Lincoln from 1834 to the end of his life.

In 1835 he wrote out a small work on Infidelity, and intended to have it published. This book was an attack upon the whole grounds of Christianity, and especially was it an attack upon the idea that Jesus was the Christ, the true and only-begotten son of God, as the Christian world contends. Mr. Lincoln was at that time in New Salem, keeping store for Mr. Samuel Hill, a merchant and postmaster of that place. Lincoln and Hill were very friendly. Hill, I think, was a skeptic at this time. Lincoln, one day after the book was finished, read it to Mr. Hill, his good friend. Hill tried to persuade him not to make it public, not to publish it. Hill at that time saw in Mr. Lincoln a rising man, and wished him success. Lincoln refused to destroy it – said it should be published. Hill swore it should never see light of day. He had an eye on Lincoln's popularity – his present and future success; and believing that if the book was published it would kill Lincoln forever, he snatched it from Lincoln's hand when Lincoln was not expecting it, and ran it into an old-fashioned tinplate stove, heated as hot as a furnace; and so Lincoln's book went up to the clouds in smoke. It is confessed by all who heard parts of it that it was at once able and eloquent; and, if I may judge of it from Mr. Lincoln's subsequent ideas and opinions, often expressed to me and to others in my presence, it was able, strong, plain, and fair. His argument was grounded on the internal mistakes of the Old and New Testaments, and on reason and on the experiences and observations of men. The criticisms from internal defects were sharp, strong, and manly.

Mr. Lincoln moved to this city in 1837, and here became acquainted with various men of his own way of thinking. At that time they called themselves Freethinkers, or free thinking men. I remember all these things distinctly; for I was with them, heard them, and was one of them. Mr. Lincoln here found other works – Hume, Gibbon, and others – and drank them in. He made no secret of his views; no concealment of his religion. He boldly avowed himself an Infidel.

When Mr. Lincoln was a candidate for our Legislature, he was accused of being an Infidel and of having said that Jesus Christ was an illegitimate child. He never denied his opinions, nor flinched from his religious views. He was a true man, and yet it may be truthfully said that in 1837 his religion was low indeed. In his moments of gloom he would doubt, if he did not sometimes deny, God.

Mr. Lincoln ran for Congress against the Rev. Peter Cartwright in the year 1846. In that contest he was accused of being an Infidel, if not an Atheist. He never denied the charge – would not – "would die first." In the first place, because he knew it could and would be proved on him; and in the second place, he was too true to his own convictions, to his own soul, to deny it.

When Mr. Lincoln left this city for Washington, I knew he had undergone no change in his religious opinions or views. He held many of the Christian ideas in abhorrence, and among them there was this one, namely, that God would forgive the sinner for a violation of his laws. Lincoln maintained that God could not forgive; that punishment has to follow the sin; that Christianity was wrong in teaching forgiveness.

From what I know of Mr. Lincoln, and from what I have heard and verily believe, I can say, first, that he did not believe in a special creation, his idea being that all creation was an evolution under law; secondly, that he did not believe that the Bible was a special revelation from God, as the Christian world contends; thirdly, he did not believe in miracles as understood by Christians; fourthly, he believed in universal inspiration and miracles under law; fifthly, he did not believe that Jesus was the Christ, the son of God, as the Christian church contends; sixthly, he believed that all things, both matter and mind, were governed by laws, universal, absolute, and eternal. All his speeches and remarks in Washington conclusively prove this. Law was to Lincoln everything, and special interferences, shams and delusions.

In 1874 Mr. Herndon delivered in Springfield a lecture on "Lincoln's Religion." It was a reply to Reed's lecture, and was published in the *State Register,* of Springfield. In this lecture he reaffirms the statements made in the "Abbott Letter," supports them with substantial arguments and proofs, and completely overthrows the claims advanced by Reed. From it I quote the following:

It is a curious fact that when any man by his genius, good fortune, or otherwise rises to public notice and to fame, it does not make much difference what life he has led, that the whole Christian world claims him as a Christian, to be forever held up to view as a hero and a saint during all the coming ages, just as if religion would die out of the soul of man unless the great dead be canonized as a model Christian. This is a species of hero or saint worship. Lincoln they are determined to enthrone among the saints, to be forever worshiped as such.

I believe that Mr. Lincoln did not late in life become a firm believer in the Christian religion. What! Mr. Lincoln discard his logical faculties and reason with his heart? What! Mr. Lincoln believe that Jesus was the Christ of God, the true and only begotten son of him, as the Christian creed contends? What! Mr. Lincoln believe that the New Testament is of special divine authority, and fully and infallibly inspired, as the Christian contends? What! Mr. Lincoln abandon his lifelong ideas of universal, eternal and absolute laws and contend that the New Testament is any more inspired than Homer's poems, than Milton's *Paradise Lost,* than Shakespeare, than his own eloquent and inspired oration at Gettysburg? What! Mr. Lincoln believe that the great Creator had connection through the form and instrumentality of a shadow with a Jewish girl? Blasphemy! These things must be believed and acknowledged in order to be a Christian.

One word concerning this discussion about Mr. Lincoln's religious views. It is important in this: 1. It settles a historic fact. 2. It makes it possible to write a true history of a man free from the fear of fire and stake. 3. It assures the reading public that the life of Mr. Lincoln will be truly written. 4. It will be a warning forever to all untrue men, that the life they have lived will be held up to view. 5. It should convince the Christian pulpit and press that it is impossible in this day and generation, at least in America, to daub up sin, and make a hero out of a fool, a knave, or a villain, which Mr. Lincoln was not. Some true spirit will drag the fraud and lie out to the light of day. 6. Its tendency will be to arrest and put a stop to romantic biographies. And now let it be written in history, and on Mr. Lincoln's tomb: "He died an unbeliever."

In January, 1883, Mr. Herndon contributed an article on "Lincoln's Religion" to the *Liberal Age,* of Milwaukee. From this article the following extracts are taken and submitted:

In 1837, Mr. Lincoln moved to the city of Springfield, and there came across many people of his own belief. They called themselves at that time Freethinkers. Some of these men were highly educated and polished gentlemen. Mr. Lincoln read in this city Hume, Gibbon, and other Liberal books. He was in this city from 1837 to 1861, an Infidel – Freethinker – Liberal – Free Religionist – of the radical type.

In his philosophy, he was a realist, as opposed to an idealist; he was a sensationalist, as opposed to an intuitionalist; and was a materialist as opposed to a spiritualist.

Some good men and women say that Mr. Lincoln was a Christian, because he was a moral man. They say that he was a *rational* Christian, because he loved morality. Do not other people, who are not Christians, love morality? Morality is not *the* test of Christianity, by any means. If it is the test, then all moral men, Atheists, Agnostics, Infidels, Mohammedans, Buddhists, Mormons, and the rest, are Christians. A *rational* Christian is an anomaly, an impossibility; because when reason is left free, it demands proofs – it relies on experience, observation, logic, nature, laws. Why not call Mr. Lincoln a rational Buddhist, a rational Mohammedan, a rational Confucian, a rational Mormon, for all these, if true to their faith, love morality.

Did Mr. Lincoln believe in prayer as a means of moving God? It is said to me by Christians, touching his religion: "Did not he, in his parting speech in Springfield, in 1861, say, 'I hope you, my friends, will pray that I may receive,' etc.?" and to which I say, yes. In his last Inaugural he said: "Fondly do we hope, fervently do we pray." These expressions are merely conventional. They do not prove that Mr. Lincoln believed that prayer is a means of moving God. . . . He believed, as I understood him, that human prayer did the prayer good; that prayer was but a drum beat – the taps of the spirit on the living human soul, arousing it to acts of repentance for bad deeds done, or to inspire it to a loftier and a higher effort for a nobler and a grander life.

Did Mr. Lincoln, in his said Inaugural, say: "Both read the same *Word of God*"? No, because that would be admitting revelation. He said: "Both read the same *Bible.*" Did Mr. Lincoln say: "Yet if God wills that it [the war] continue till all the wealth piled by the bondman's two hundred and fifty years of unrequited toil shall be sunk, and until every drop of blood drawn by the lash shall be paid with another drawn by the sword, *as was said by God* three thousand years ago"? He did not; he was cautious, and said: "*As was said* three thousand years ago." Jove never nods.

A little later Mr. Herndon wrote an article entitled, "Abraham Lincoln's Religious Belief," which appeared in the *Truth Seeker* of New York. From this article I quote the following passages:

In 1842 I heard Mr. Lincoln deliver a speech before the Washingtonian Temperance Society, of this city. . . . He scorned the Christians for the position they had taken. He said in that lecture this: "If they [the Christians] believe, as they profess – that Omnipotence condescended to take on himself the form of sinful man," etc. This was spoken with energy. He scornfully and contemptuously emphasized the words *as they profess.* The rebuke was as much in the manner of utterance as in the substance of what was said. I heard the criticisms of some of the Christians that night. They said the speech was an insult and an outrage.

It is my opinion that no man ever heard Mr. Lincoln pray, in the true evangelical sense of that word. His philosophy is against all human prayer, as a means of reversing God's decrees.

He has told me often that there was no freedom in the human will, and no punishment beyond this world. He denied God's higher law, and wrote on the margin of a newspaper to his friends in the Chicago convention in 1860, this: "Lincoln agrees with Seward in his irrepressible-conflict idea; but he is opposed to Seward's *higher law.*" This paper was handed to Judge Davis, Judge Logan, and other friends.

Mr. Lincoln and a minister, whose name is kept in the dark, had a conversation about religion. It appears that Mr. Lincoln said. that when his son – bone of his bone, flesh of his flesh, and blood of his own heart – died, though a severe affliction, it did not arouse him to think of Christ; but when he saw the graves of so many soldiers – strangers to him – that sad sight aroused him to love Jesus. . . . It is a fine thing for the reputation of the "Illinois Clergyman" that his name is to the world unknown. It is a most heartless thing, this supposed conversation of Lincoln with the Illinois clergyman. What! Lincoln feel more for the *graves* of strangers than for the death of his once living, loving, and lovable son, now dead, moldering to ashes in the silent tomb! The charge is barbarous. To make Lincoln a lover of Jesus, whom he once ridiculed, this minister makes him a savage.

I wish to give an illustration of the uncertainty and unreliability of those loose things that float around in the newspapers of the day, and how liable things are to be inaccurate – so made even by the best of men. Mr. Lincoln on the morning he started for Washington to take the oath of office, and be inaugurated President of this great Republic, gave a short farewell address to his old friends. It was eloquent and touching. That speech is copied in Holland's *Life of Lincoln*, in Arnold's *Lincoln and Slavery*, and in Lamon's *Life of Lincoln*, and no two are exactly alike. If it is hard to get the exact truth on such an occasion as this, how impossible is it to get at Mr. Lincoln's sayings which have been written out by men weeks and months after what he did say have passed by! All these loose and foolish things that Mr. Lincoln is supposed to have said are like the

cords of driftwood, floating on the bosom of the great Missis-
sippi, down to the great gulf of – Forgetfulness. Let them go.

Herndon's *Life of Lincoln* is a most important contribution to biographical literature. It will enable the present and future generations to become better acquainted with Lincoln the
man than with any other prominent American. The author has
performed substantially the same work for Lincoln that Boswell
performed for Johnson; only he has performed it more faithfully.
Political partisans and religious bigots may condemn the work,
but impartial critics are almost unanimous in their praise of it.

The metropolitan journals of Lincoln's and Herndon's own
State commend the work. The *Chicago Tribune* says: "All these
loving adherents [of Lincoln] will hail Herndon's *Lincoln* with
unmixed, unbounded joy." The *Chicago Times* says: "Herndon's
Life is the best yet written." The *Inter Ocean* says that Herndon
"knew more of Lincoln's inner life than any living man." The
Chicago Herald says: "It enables one to approach more closely
to the great President." The *Chicago Evening Journal* says: "It
presents a truthful and living picture of the greatest of Americans."

The *Nation* thus refers to it: "The sincerity and honesty
of the biographer appear on every page." The *New York Sun*
says: "The marks of unflinching veracity are patent in every
line." The *Washington Capital* says that it places "Lincoln before
the world as he really was." The *Commercial Gazette,* of
Cincinnati, says: "He describes the life of his friend Lincoln just
as he saw it." The *Morning Call*, of San Francisco, affirms that
it "contains the only true history of the lamented President." The
St. Louis Republic says: "It will do more to shape the judgment
of posterity on Mr. Lincoln's character than all that has been
written or will be hereafter written."

In this work Mr. Herndon states in brief the substance of
the articles already quoted in this chapter I quote as follows:

No man had a stronger or firmer faith in Providence –
God – than Mr. Lincoln, but the continued use by him late in life
of the word *God* must not be interpreted to mean that he believed
in a personal God. In 1854 he asked me to erase the word *God*

from a speech which I had written and read to him for criticism, because my language indicated a personal God, whereas he insisted that no such personality ever existed.

The world has always insisted on making an orthodox Christian of him, and to analyze his language or sound his belief is but to break the idol.

The benevolence of his impulses, the seriousness of his convictions, and the nobility of his character, are evidences unimpeachable that his soul was ever filled with the exalted purity and the sublime faith of natural religion.[3]

---

3. *Life of Lincoln*, pp. 445, 446.

CHAPTER SIX:
Testimony of Hon. William H. Herndon –
Unpublished Testimony
☆　☆　☆　☆

Extracts from Herndon's Letters – The Books Lincoln Read
His Philosophy – His Infidelity – Refutation of Christian Claims
Attempts to Invalidate Herndon's Testimony – Reed's Calumnies
Vindication

In the preceding chapter has been submitted the evidence of Mr. Herndon that has already been published. In this chapter will be presented some hitherto unpublished testimony.

The writer corresponded with Mr. Herndon for many years. Much of this correspondence related to Abraham Lincoln, and no inconsiderable portion of it to the subject under consideration. Permission was granted by Mr. Herndon to use such parts of this correspondence as may be deemed of value. The limits of this work preclude the presentation of much that is really interesting, but no apology is needed for devoting space to the following extracts from his letters, written at various intervals between 1880 and 1890:

> I was the personal friend of Mr. Lincoln from 1834 to the day of his death. In 1843 we entered into a partnership which was never formally dissolved. When he became unpopular in this Congressional district because of his speeches on the Mexican war, I was faithful to him. When he espoused the antislavery cause and in the eyes of most men had hopelessly ruined his political prospects, I stood by him, and through the press defended his course. In these dark hours, by our unity of sentiment and by political ostracism we were driven to a close

and enduring friendship. You should take it for granted, then, that I knew Mr. Lincoln well, During all this time, from 1834 to 1862, when I last saw him, he never intimated to me, either directly or indirectly, that he had changed his religious opinions. Had he done so – had he let drop one word or look in that direction, I should have detected it.

I had an excellent private library, probably the best in the city for admired books. To this library Mr. Lincoln had, as a matter of course, full and free access at all times. I purchased such books as Locke, Kant, Fichte, Lewes; Sir Wm. Hamilton's *Discussions on Philosophy*; Spencer's *First Principles*, *Social Statics*, etc.; Buckle's *History of Civilization*, and Lecky's *History of Rationalism*. I also possessed the works of Parker, Paine, Emerson, and Strauss; Gregg's *Creed of Christendom*, McNaught on Inspiration, Volney's *Ruins*, Feuerbach's *Essence of Christianity*, and other works on Infidelity. Mr. Lincoln read some of these works. About the year 1843 he borrowed *The Vestiges of Creation* of Mr. James W. Keys, of this city, and read it carefully. He subsequently read the sixth edition of this work, which I loaned him. Mr. Lincoln had always denied special creation, but from his want of education he did not know just what to believe. He adopted the progressive and development theory as taught more or less directly in that work. He despised speculation, especially in the metaphysical world. He was purely a practical man. He adopted Locke's notions as his system of mental philosophy, with some modifications to suit his own views. He held that reason drew her inferences as to law, etc., from observation, experience, and reflection on the facts and phenomena of nature. He was a pure sensationalist, except as above. He was a materialist in his philosophy. He denied dualism, and at times immortality in any sense.

Before I wrote my Abbott letter I diligently searched through Lincoln's letters, speeches, state papers, etc., to find the word *immortality,* and I could not find it anywhere except in his letter to his father. The word *immortality* appears but once in his writings.

If he had been asked the plain question, "Do you *know* that a God exists?" he would have said: "I do *not know* that a God exists."

At one moment of his life I know that he was an Atheist. I was preparing a speech on Kansas, and in it, like nearly all reformers, I invoked *God.* He made me wipe out that word and substitute the word *Maker,* affirming that said Maker was a principle of the universe. When he went to Washington he did the same to a friend there.

Mr. Lincoln told me, over and over, that man has no freedom of will, or, as he termed it, "No man has a freedom of mind." He was in one sense a fatalist, and so died. He believed that he was under the thumb of Providence (which to him was but another name for fate). The longer he lived the more firmly he believed it, and hence his oft invocations of God. But these invocations are no evidence to a rational mind that he adopted the blasphemy that God seduced his own daughter, begat a son on purpose to have mankind kill him, in order that he, God, might become reconciled to his own mistakes, according to the Christian view.

Lincoln would wait patiently on the flow and logic of events. He believed that conditions make the man and not man the conditions. Under his own hand he says: "I attempt no compliment to my own sagacity. I claim not to have controlled events, but confess plainly that events have controlled me." He believed in the supreme reign of law. This law *fated* things, as he would express it. Now, how could a man be a Christian – could believe that Jesus Christ was God – could believe in the efficacy of prayer – and entertain such a belief?

He did not believe in the efficacy of prayer, although he used that conventional language. He said in Washington, "God has his own purposes." If God has his own purposes, then prayer will not change God's purposes.

I have often said to you, and now repeat it, that Lincoln was a scientific Materialist, *i.e.,* that this was his tendency as opposed to the Spiritualistic idea. Lincoln always contended that general and universal laws ruled the universe – always did – do now – and ever will. He was an Agnostic generally, sometimes an Atheist.

That Mr. Lincoln was an Infidel from 1834 to 1861, I know, and that he remained one to the day of his death, I honestly believe. I always understood that he was an Infidel, sometimes bordering on Atheism. I never saw any change in the man, and the change could not have escaped my observation had it happened.

Lincoln's task was a terrible one. When he took the oath of office his soul was bent on securing harmony among all the people of the North, and so he chose for his Cabinet officers his opponents for the Presidential candidacy in order and as a means of creating a united North. He let all parties, professions, and callings have their way where their wishes did not cut across his own. He was apparently pliant and supple. He ruled men when men thought they were ruling him. He often said to me that the Christian religion was a dangerous element to deal with when aroused. He saw in the Kansas affairs – in the whole history of slavery, in fact – its rigor and encroachments, that Christianity was aroused. It must be controlled, and that in the right direction. Hence he bent to it, fed it, and kept it within bounds, well knowing that it would crush his administration to atoms unless appeased. His oft and oft invocations of God, his conversations with Christians, his apparent respect for Christianity, etc., were all means to an end. And yet sometimes he showed that he hated its nasal whines.

A gentleman of veracity in Washington told me this story. and vouched for its truthfulness: "A tall saddle-faced man," said he, "came to Washington to pray with Lincoln, having declared this to be his intention at the hotel. About 10 o'clock A.M. the bloodless man, dressed in black with white cravat, went to the White House, sent in his card, and was admitted. Lincoln glanced at the man and knew his motives in an instant. He said to him angrily: 'What, have you, too, come to torment me with your prayers?' The man was squelched – said, 'No, Mr. Lincoln' – lied out and out. Lincoln spoiled those prayers."

Mr. Lincoln was thought to be understood by the mob. But what a delusion! He was one of the most reticent men that ever lived. All of us – Stuart, Speed, Logan, Matheny, myself, and others– had to guess at much of the man. He was a mystery to the world – a sphinx to most men. One peculiarity of Mr. Lincoln was his irritability when anyone tried to peep into his own mind's laboratory. Considering all this, what can be thought of the stories about what he is said to have confided to strangers in regard to his religion?

Not one of Lincoln's old acquaintances in this city ever

heard of his conversion to Christianity by Dr. Smith or anyone else. It was never suggested nor thought of here until after his death.

I never saw him read a second of time in Dr. Smith's book on Infidelity. He threw it down upon our table – spit upon it as it were – and never opened it to my knowledge.

My opinion is, from what I have heard and know, that these men – Gurley and Simpson – refused to be a party to a fraud on the public touching Lincoln's religion. I think that they understood each other the day that the remains of Lincoln were put to rest.

Holland came into my office, in 1865, and asked me this question: "What about Mr. Lincoln's Christianity?" To this, I replied: "The less said about it the better." Holland then said to me, "Oh, never mind, I'll fix that," and went over to Bateman and had it fixed.

Lincoln never revealed to Judge Davis, Judge Matheny, Joshua F. Speed, Joseph Gillespie, nor myself that he was a Christian, or that he had a change of heart, or anything like it, at any time. Now, taking into consideration the fact that he was one of the most non-communicative of men – that Bateman was, as it were, a mere stranger to him – that Bateman was frightened, excited, conscience-smitten when I approached him on the subject, and that in after years he confessed to me that his notes in Holland's *Life of Lincoln* were *colored* – taking all this into consideration, I say, can you believe Bateman's story to be true?

I see quoted frequently a supposed speech made by Mr. Lincoln to the colored people of Baltimore, on the presentation of a Bible to him. This supposed speech contains the following: "All the good from the Savior of the world is communicated to us through this book." This idea is false and foolish. What becomes of nine-tenths of the life of Jesus of which we have no history – nine-tenths of the great facts of this grand man's life not recorded in this book? Mr. Lincoln was full and exact in his language. He never used the word Savior, unless in a conventional sense; in fact, he never used the word at all. Again, he is made to say: "But for this book we could not know right from wrong." The lowest organized life, I was about to say, knows right from wrong in its particular sphere. Every good dog that comes into possession of a bone, knows that that bone belongs to him, and he knows that it is wrong for another dog to rob him of it. He protests with bristling hair and glistening teeth against such dog robbery. It requires no revelation to teach him right from wrong in the dog world; yet it requires a special revelation from God to teach us right from wrong in the human world. According to this speech, the dog has the advantage. But Mr. Lincoln never uttered such nonsense.

I do think that anyone who knew Mr. Lincoln — his history — his philosophy — his opinions — and still asserts that he was a Christian, is an unbounded falsifier. I hate to speak thus plainly, but I cannot respect an untruthful man.

Let me ask the Christian claimant a few questions. Do you mean to say, when you assert that Mr. Lincoln was a Christian, that he believed that Jesus was the Christ of God, as the evangelical world contends? If so, where do you get your information? Do you mean to say that Mr. Lincoln was a converted man and that he so declared? If so where, when, and before whom did he declare or reveal it? Do you mean to say that Mr. Lincoln joined a church? If so, what church did he join, and when did he join it? Do you mean to say that Mr. Lincoln was a secret Christian, acting under the cloak of the devil to advance Christianity? If so, what is your authority? If you will tell me when it was that the Creator caught with his almighty arms, Abraham, and held him fast while he poured the oil of grace on his rebellious soul, then I will know when it was that he was converted from his Infidel views to Christianity.

The best evidence this side of Lincoln's own written statement that he was an Infidel, if not an Atheist, as claimed by some, is the fact that he never mentions the name of Jesus. If he was a Christian it could be proved by his letters and speeches. That man is a poor defender of a principle, of a person, or of a thing, who never mentions that principle, person, or thing. I have never seen the name of Jesus mentioned by Mr. Lincoln.

Mr. Lincoln never mentioned the name of Christ in his letters and speeches as a Christian. I have searched for such evidence, but could not find it. I have had others search, but they could not find it. This dead silence on the part of Mr. Lincoln is overwhelming proof that he was an unbeliever.

While Lincoln frequently, in a conventional way, appeals to God, he never appeals to Christ nor mentions him. I know that he at first maintained that Jesus was a bastard, and later that he was the son of Joseph and not of God.

Lincoln was not a Christian in any sense other than that he lived a good life and was a noble man. If a good life constitutes one a Christian, then Mill and a million other men who repudiated and denied Christianity were Christians, for they lived good and noble lives.

If Mr. Lincoln changed his religious views he owed it to me to warn me, as he above all other men caused me to be an unbeliever. He said nothing to me, intimated nothing to me, either directly or indirectly. He owed this debt to many young men whom he had led astray, if astray the Christian calls it. I know of two young men of promise, now dead and gone – gone into endless misery, according to the evangelical creed – caused by Mr. Lincoln's teachings. I know some of the living here, men in prominent positions of life, who were made unbelievers by him.

One by one, these apocryphal stories go by the board. Courageous and remorseless criticism will wipe out all these things. There will not be a vestige of them in fifty years to laugh at or to weep at.

Mr. Herndon's testimony, even in the absence of all other evidence, is conclusive. This was recognized by the Christian claimants after the appearance of his "Abbott Letter." They employed various measures to break the force of his testimony by trying to induce him either to retract or modify his statements. But they were not successful. He was not to be coaxed, he was not to be purchased, he was not to be intimidated. He had stated the truth and by the truth he proposed to stand. Foiled in these efforts, their last resort was to destroy his credibility as a witness by destroying his character. The most brazen falsehoods were invented and the most cruel calumnies circulated in order to crush him. Some of these stated that he was a drunkard, others that he was a pauper, and still others that he had become insane.

These defamatory statements were usually first noticed in some religious paper or periodical. From this they were naturally copied into the secular papers and sent broadcast over the land.

Journalists who had once known Mr. Herndon, either personally or by reputation, were surprised and shocked at the announcements, and wrote articles like the following which appeared in a Kansas paper:

> Bill Herndon is a pauper in Springfield, Ill. He was once worth considerable property. His mind was the most argumentative of any of the old lawyers in the state, and his memory was extraordinary. For several years before Lincoln was nominated for the Presidency, Herndon was in some respects the most active member of the firm, preparing the greatest number of cases for trial and making elaborate arguments in their behalf. It is said that he worked hard with Lincoln in preparing the memorable speeches delivered by the man who afterward became President, during the debates between Lincoln and Douglas in 1858, and in constructing the Cooper Institute address delivered by Lincoln a short time before the war. Herndon, with all his attainments, was a man who now and then went on a spree. This habit became worse after Lincoln's death, and, like poor Dick Yates, he went down step by step till his old friends and associates point to him as a common drunkard.

I was in Springfield the very week that this article was published, and passed a day with Mr. Herndon at his home. I was prepared to testify, as all his neighbors were, that the charges it contained, together with others that were being circulated, were false. I knew that he still possessed a sound and vigorous intellect; I knew that he was in comfortable circumstances financially; I knew that he was an earnest advocate of temperance, and that he practiced what he preached; in short, I knew him to be a man of pure morals and exemplary character. At the very time that he was declared to be an inmate of the insane asylum, the Old Settlers' Society selected him to examine and report upon the correctness of the *History of Sangamon County*, which, as it included a history of the capital of the State where, at one time or another, had resided a majority of Illinois's most gifted sons, was an important work, and one whose revision would not likely be intrusted to a lunatic. At the very time that he was said to be a pauper in the county poorhouse, he was entertaining such distinguished guests as William Lloyd Garrison. At the very time that he was reported to be a common drunkard, his neighbors had just appointed him guardian of the educational interests of their children.

All efforts to trace these slanders to their source and discover their author proved futile until 1880, when the writer of this saw in an Ohio paper an article on Lincoln, in which was quoted a portion of a letter which the contributor of the article stated had just been received from the Rev. J. A. Reed, of Springfield. It related wholly to Mr. Herndon, and did not contain one fair, truthful statement. In thirty brief lines were concentrated, in addition to several statements calculated and intended to deceive, no less than sixteen deliberate falsehoods – some of them of the most cruel and infamous character. It was evident that Reed had intended that the substance of his letter should be given to the public without disclosing its authorship. But, thanks to the innocent credulity and indiscreetness of the friend to whom it was sent, the defamer was discovered and exposed. And this sneaking, cowardly assassin was the "defender of Lincoln's Christian faith"! Could the inanimate remains of Abraham Lincoln have been revivified when this exposure was made, he would have arisen from his mausoleum at Oak Ridge, have come into the city, and have kicked this pretended "defender," this base calumniator of his beloved friend and associate, out of Springfield.

The cause of all the vituperation which for years had been heaped upon Mr. Herndon was now apparent. He had replied to Reed's lecture, and openly, honestly, and courteously, but effectively, refuted it and because the latter could not come forward with a successful rejoinder, he was thus heartlessly and covertly plunging a dagger into the reputation of his chivalrous opponent. The intercession of friends secured for the culprit immunity from arrest for libel, but in the newspapers of his city he received such a castigation as he will not soon forget. The *Daily Monitor,* in an editorial replying to the slanders that were being circulated concerning Mr. Herndon, said:

Mr. Herndon is not a pauper, is not a drunkard; whisky

did not ruin him, and, in a word, the whole thing is a lie. Mr. Herndon lives on his farm near this city. He is a great admirer of nature, loves flowers, and spends his whole time on the farm, except when doing his trading, or coming into the city to see his children and grandchildren. He don't drink, he don't chew tobacco, he don't gamble, he is honorable and truthful, and he is highly respected by his fellow-citizens. He is a great reader, a great thinker, loves his neighbors and his neighbors love him. He has a great, big, kind heart for his fellowman in distress, and, while never worth "considerable property," he has always had enough for his generous purposes. Just why this thing should be allowed we are at a loss to know, and have waited to see if some of those who profess so much of the Christ-like in their composition would not have enough of the man-like to be men, and not allow a good and true man as Mr. Herndon is to be thus infamously maligned and belied by those whose works in the salvation of men would have more effect if more akin to Christ in practice.

After a life of honest toil, much of it in behalf of the poor and the weak, without reward and without the expectation of reward, to be in his old age thus shamefully robbed of his good name, was an outrage almost without a parallel, save in the treatment received by Thomas Paine. That Mr. Herndon was keenly sensitive to this great wrong is disclosed by the tone of his letters written at the time. In one he says:

> I have done nothing in the spirit of self-laudation. I prefer moving down the grooves of time unnoticed and unknown, except to friends. I have no ambition for fame or money. My ambition is to try to do good. I spent ten or more years of my best life for the negro, liberty, and union, not forgetting Kansas and her brave people. But let it all go; I make no complaint. I try to live a moral and a manly life, love my fellow man, love freedom, love justice, and would die for the eternal right.

As an index of public sentiment in the community where the defamed and the defamer resided, I will state two facts. On a pleasant September evening, in 1882, I attended Dr. Reed's church in Springfield. In that commodious edifice, built to accommodate an audience of nearly one thousand, I found assembled to listen to this renowned "defender of Lincoln's Christian faith," an audience of forty-four persons. About the same time, in the published report of a public meeting held near Springfield, appeared the following: "Five thousand people hovered around the speaker's stand for the purpose of listening to the able, eloquent, and well-known Hon. W.H. Herndon."

It has been charged that Mr. Herndon's statements concerning Lincoln's unbelief were inspired by a spirit of revenge in consequence of Lincoln's not having recognized him with an appointment. This charge and this assumption are both false. There is now on file at Washington and at Springfield a telegram from Lincoln tendering him a judgeship, which he declined.

To know Lincoln was to love him. None knew him better than Mr. Herndon, and none entertained a deeper affection for his memory. In a letter to me, dated Nov. 4, 1881, he pays this tribute to his dead friend:

> Some people say that Mr. Lincoln was an ungrateful man. This is not true, and especially when applied to myself. He was always kind, tender, and grateful to me – clung to me with hooks of steel. I know that I was true to him. It is said that no man is great to his valet. If I was Mr. Lincoln's valet, the rule does not apply in this case, for my opinion of him is too well known. His was a grand, noble, true, and manly life. He dreamed dreams of glory, and glory was justly his. He was growing and expanding to the day of his death. He was slow in his development, but strong and big when he did come. The last letter which I ever received from him concluded thus: "God bless you, says your friend. *A. Lincoln.*" He felt what he expressed, and in return I say, *God bless you, Lincoln.*

CHAPTER SEVEN
Testimony of Col. Ward H. Lamon
☆   ☆   ☆   ☆

Lamon's *Life of Lincoln* – Lincoln's Early Skepticism
His Investigations at New Salem – His Book on Infidelity
His Religious Opinions Remain Unchanged – Holland's
Condemnation of Lamon's Work – Holland's and Lamon's
Works Compared

In 1872, seven years after the President's assassination, appeared the *Life of Abraham Lincoln*, written by Col. Ward H. Lamon. As a faithful record of the life of one of the most sublime characters in the world's history, this work stands unrivaled. More accomplished writers have written biography – have written the biography of Lincoln. But no writer has ever been more thoroughly informed respecting his subject, and no writer has ever made a more conscientious use of the information in his possession than has Colonel Lamon in his *Life of Lincoln*. In Illinois he was the friend and confidant of Lincoln. When the time approached for Lincoln to take the Executive chair, and the journey from Springfield to Washington was deemed a dangerous undertaking, to Colonel Lamon was intrusted the responsible duty of conducting him to the national capital. During the eventful years that followed, he remained at the President's side, holding an important official position in the District of Columbia. When Lincoln died, at the great funeral pageant in Washington, he led the civic procession, and was, with Major General Hunter and Judge David Davis, selected to convey the remains to their final resting-place at Springfield.

The following extract, from the preface to his work, shows what an inexhaustible mine of materials he had with which to prepare a full and authentic record of Lincoln's life and character:

At the time of Mr. Lincoln's death, I determined to write his history, as I had in my possession much valuable material for such a purpose. . . . Early in 1869, Mr. Herndon placed at my disposal his remarkable collection of materials – the richest, rarest, and fullest collection it was possible to conceive. . . . Mr. Herndon had been the partner in business and the intimate personal associate of Mr. Lincoln for something like a quarter of a century; and Mr. Lincoln had lived familiarly with several members of his family long before their individual acquaintance began. New Salem, Springfield, the old judicial circuit, the habits and friends of Mr. Lincoln, were as well known to Mr. Herndon as to himself. With these advantages, and from the numberless facts and hints which had dropped from Mr. Lincoln during the confidential intercourse of an ordinary lifetime, Mr. Herndon was able to institute a thorough system of inquiry for every noteworthy circumstance and every incident of value in Mr. Lincoln's career. The fruits of Mr. Herndon's labors are garnered in three enormous volumes of original manuscripts and a mass of unarranged letters and papers. They comprise the recollections of Mr. Lincoln's nearest friends; of the surviving members of his family and his family-connections; of the men still living who knew him and his parents in Kentucky; of his schoolfellows, neighbors, and acquaintances in Indiana; of the better part of the whole population of New Salem; of his associates and relatives at Springfield; and of lawyers, judges, politicians, and statesmen everywhere, who had anything of interest or moment to relate. They were collected at vast expense of time, labor, and money, involving the employment of many agents, long journeys, tedious examinations, and voluminous correspondence. Upon the value of these materials it would be impossible to place an estimate. That I have used them conscientiously and justly is the only merit to which I lay claim.

Lamon's evidence concerning Lincoln's unbelief is complete and unanswerable. He did not present it because he was himself an unbeliever and wished to support his views with the prestige of Lincoln's great name. While the Freethinker regards Lincoln's rejection of Christianity as in the highest degree meritorious – a proof of his strong logical acumen, his sterling common sense, and his broad humanity – Lamon considered it a grave defect in his character. He states the fact because it is a fact, and because the purpose of his work is to disclose and not conceal the facts of Lincoln's life. If he devotes considerable space to the subject, and exhibits a special earnestness in its presentation, the misrepresentations of Lincoln's Christian biographers have furnished a reasonable pretext for it.

In the pages immediately following will be given the individual testimony of Colonel Lamon:

> Any analysis of Mr. Lincoln's character would be defective that did not include his religious opinions. On such matters he thought deeply, and his opinions were positive. But perhaps no phase of his character has been more persistently misrepresented and variously misunderstood, than this of his religious belief. Not that the conclusive testimony of many of his intimate associates relative to his frequent expressions on such subjects has ever been wanting; but his great prominence in the world's history, and his identification with some of the great questions of our time, which, by their moral import, were held to be eminently religious in their character, have led many good people to trace in his motives and actions similar convictions to those held by themselves. His extremely general expressions of religious faith called forth by the grave exigencies of his public life, or indulged in on occasions of private condolence, have too often been distorted out of relation to their real significance or meaning to suit the opinions or tickle the fancies of individuals or parties.
>
> Mr. Lincoln was never a member of any church, nor did he believe in the divinity of Christ, or the inspiration of the Scriptures in the sense understood by evangelical Christians.[1]

---

1. *Life of Lincoln*, p. 486.

Holland and other Christian biographers have represented Lincoln as a youth of extreme piety, whose constant companion was the Bible. The concurrent testimony of the friends of his boyhood compels Colonel Lamon to affirm that the reverse of this is true that Lincoln, at an early age, was noted for his skepticism. He says:

> At an early age he began to attend the "preachings" roundabout, but principally at the Pigeon Creek church, with a view to catching whatever might be ludicrous in the preacher's air or matter, and making it the subject of mimicry as soon as he could collect an audience of idle boys and men to hear him. A pious stranger, passing that way on a Sunday morning, was invited to preach for the Pigeon Creek congregation; but he banged the boards of the old pulpit, and bellowed and groaned so wonderfully, that Abe could hardly contain his mirth. This memorable sermon was a great favorite with him; and he frequently reproduced it with nasal tones, rolling eyes, and all manner of droll aggravations, to the great delight of Nat Grigsby and the wild fellows whom Nat was able to assemble. . . .
>
> His chronicles were many, and on a great variety of subjects. They were written, as his early admirers love to tell us, "in the Scriptural style;" but those we have betray a very limited acquaintance with the model. . . .
>
> When a boy, he showed no sign of that piety which his many biographers ascribe to his manhood. When he went to church at all, he went to mock, and came away to mimic. . . .[2]

Of his Freethought reading and theological investigations at New Salem, and his book on Infidelity, Lamon says:

> The community in which he lived was preeminently a community of Freethinkers in matters of religion; and it was then no secret, nor has it been a secret since, that Mr. Lincoln agreed with the majority of his associates in denying to the Bible the authority of divine revelation. It was his honest belief, a belief which it was no reproach to hold at New Salem, Anno Domini 1834, and one which he never thought of concealing. It

---

2. *Ibid.*, pp. 55, 63, 486, 487.

was no distinction, either good or bad, no honor, and no shame. But he had made himself thoroughly familiar with the writings of Volney and Paine – the *Ruins* by the one, and *The Age of Reason* by the other. His mind was full of the subject, and he felt an itching to write. He did write, and the result was a little book. It was probably merely an extended essay, but it is ambitiously spoken of as "a book" by himself and by the persons who were made acquainted with its contents. In this work he intended to demonstrate –

"First, that the Bible was not God's revelation; Secondly, that Jesus was not the son of God."

No leaf of this little volume has survived. Mr. Lincoln carried it in manuscript to the store of Mr. Samuel Hill, where it was read and discussed. Hill was himself an unbeliever, but his son considered his book "infamous." It is more than probable that Hill, being a warm personal friend of Lincoln, feared that the publication of the essay would some day interfere with the political advancement of his favorite. At all events, he snatched it out of his hand, and thrust it into the fire, from which not a shred escaped. . . .

When he came to New Salem, he consorted with Freethinkers, joined with them in deriding the gospel history of Jesus, read Volney and Paine, and then wrote a deliberate and labored essay, wherein he reached conclusions similar to theirs. The essay was burnt, but he never denied or regretted its composition. On the contrary, he made it the subject of free and frequent conversations with his friends at Springfield, and stated, with much particularity and precision, the origin, arguments, and objects of the work.[3]

Colonel Lamon is confident that while Lincoln finally ceased to openly promulgate his Freethought opinions, he never abandoned them. He says:

As he grew older, he grew more cautious; and as his New Salem associates, and the aggressive Deists with whom he originally united at Springfield, gradually dispersed, or fell away from his side, he appreciated more and more keenly the

---

3. *Ibid.*, pp. 157, 158, 487.

violence and extent of the religious prejudices which freedom in discussion from his standpoint would be sure to arouse against him. He saw the immense and augmenting power of the churches, and in times past had practically felt it. The imputation of Infidelity had seriously injured him in several of his earlier political contests; and, sobered by age and experience, he was resolved that that same imputation should injure him no more. Aspiring to lead religious communities, he foresaw that he must not appear as an enemy within their gates; aspiring to public honors under the auspices of a political party which persistently summoned religious people to assist in the extirpation of that which is denounced as the 'nation's sin,' he foresaw that he could not ask their suffrages whilst aspersing their faith. He perceived no reason for changing his convictions, but he did perceive many good and cogent reasons for not making them public. . . .

But he never told anyone that he accepted Jesus as the Christ, or performed a single one of the acts which necessarily follow upon such a conviction. At Springfield and at Washington he was beset on the one hand by political priests, and on the other by honest and prayerful Christians. He despised the former, respected the latter, and had use for both. He said with characteristic irreverence that he would not undertake to "run the churches by military authority;" but he was, nevertheless, alive to the importance of letting the churches "run" themselves in the interest of his party. Indefinite expressions about "Divine Providence," the "Justice of God," "the favor of the Most High," were easy, and not inconsistent with his religious notions. In this, accordingly, he indulged freely; but never in all that time did he let fall from his lips or his pen an expression which remotely implied the slightest faith in Jesus as the son of God and the Savior of men.[4]

Lamon was Lincoln's intimate and trusted friend at Washington, and had he changed his belief, his biographer, as well as Noah Brooks and the Illinois clergyman, would have been in possession of the fact.

---

4. *Ibid.*, pp. 497, 498, 502.

In 1851 Lincoln wrote a letter of consolation to his dying father, in which he counseled him to "confide in our great and good and merciful Maker." This letter was given to the public by Mr. Herndon, and has been cited by the orthodox to prove that Lincoln was a believer. Adverting to this letter Lamon says:

> If ever there was a moment when Mr. Lincoln might have been expected to express his faith in the atonement, his trust in the merits of a living Redeemer, it was when he undertook to send a composing and comforting message to a dying man. But he omitted it wholly. He did not even mention the name of Jesus, or intimate the most distant suspicion of the existence of a Christ.[5]

Lincoln's mind was not entirely free from superstition, but though born and reared in Christendom, the superstitious element in his nature was not essentially Christian. His fatalistic ideas, so characteristic of the faith of Islam, have already been mentioned by Mr. Herndon, and are thus referred to by Colonel Lamon:

> His mind was filled with gloomy forebodings and strong apprehensions of impending evil, mingled with extravagant visions of personal grandeur and power. His imagination painted a scene just beyond the veil of the immediate future, gilded with glory yet tarnished with blood. It was his "destiny" – splendid but dreadful, fascinating but terrible. His case bore little resemblance to those of religious enthusiasts like Bunyan, Cowper, and others. His was more like the delusion of the fatalist conscious of his star. . . .
>
> Mr. Lincoln was by no means free from a kind of belief in the supernatural. . . . He lived constantly in the serious conviction that he was himself the subject of a special decree, made by some unknown and mysterious power, for which he had no name.[6]

---

5. *Ibid.*, p. 497.

6. *Ibid.*, pp. 475, 503.

When Lamon's work appeared, Holland, backed by the Christian element generally, fell upon it like a savage and sought, as far as possible, to suppress it. Lamon had committed an unpardonable offense. He had declared to the world that Lincoln had died a disbeliever, and, what was worse, he had proved it. Holland's attack was made in an eight-column review of Lamon's *Life,* which was published in *Scribner's Monthly,* for August, 1872. In order to give an air of candor and judicial fairness to his venomous criticisms, he opens with this flattering recognition of its merits:

> It is not difficult to see how Colonel Lamon, who during Mr. Lincoln's Presidency held an office in the District of Columbia, which must have brought him into somewhat frequent intercourse with the President, and who, indeed, had come with him from Springfield to the Capital, should feel that there rested on him a certain biographical duty. And certainly he was in possession of a mass of material so voluminous, so original, and so fresh that in this respect at least his fitness for the work was remarkably complete. Moreover, Mr. W.H. Herndon, who was Mr. Lincoln's partner in the practice of the law at Springfield, and was, of course, closely intimate with his partner in a business way, . . . added to Colonel Lamon's material the valuable documents which he had himself collected, and the memoranda which, with painstaking and lawyer-like ability, he had recorded from the oral testimony of living witnesses.
> As far as the story of Mr. Lincoln's childhood and early life is concerned, down to the time when his political life began, it has never been told so fully, with such spirit and zest, and with such evident accuracy, as by Colonel Lamon.

Nearly the entire review is devoted to a denunciation of Lamon's exposition of Lincoln's religious opinions. He repeatedly pronounces this "an outrage on decency," and characterizes Lincoln's Freethought companions as "heathen," "barbarians," and "savages." The review concludes as follows:

> The violent and reckless prejudice, and the utter want of delicacy and even of decency by which the book is character-

ized, in such instances as this, will more than counterbalance
the value of its new material, its fresh and vigorous pictures of
Western life and manners, and its familiar knowledge of the
inside politics of Mr. Lincoln's administration, and will even
make its publication (by the famous publishers whose imprint
imparts to it a prestige and authority which its authorship would
fail to give) something like a national misfortune. In some quar-
ters it will be readily received as the standard life of the good
President. It is all the more desirable that the criticism upon it
should be prompt and unsparing.

Christianity must have the support of Lincoln's great
name. To secure it Holland is willing to misrepresent the honest
convictions of Lincoln's lifetime, to traduce the characters of his
dearest friends, and to rob a brother author and a publisher of
their just reward.

Lamon states that during the last years of Lincoln's life
he ceased to proclaim his Infidel opinions because they were
unpopular. Referring to this statement, Holland says: "The eagerness with which this volume strives to cover Mr. Lincoln's memory with an imputation so detestable is one of the most pitiable
exhibitions which we have lately witnessed."

This outburst of righteous indignation, coming from the
source it does, is peculiarly refreshing. To appreciate it, we have
only to open Holland's work, and read such passages as the following:

> I am obliged to appear different to them. . . . It was one
> of the peculiarities of Mr. Lincoln to hide these religious
> [Christian] experiences from the eyes of the world. . . . Who had
> never in their whole lives heard from his lips one word of all these
> religious convictions and experiences. . . . They [his friends] did
> not regard him as a religious man. . . . All this department of his
> life he had kept carefully hidden from them. . . . There was much
> of his conduct that was simply a cover to these thoughts an effort
> to conceal them.[7]

---

7. Holland's *Life of Lincoln*, pp. 239, 240.

Consummate hypocrisy in a Christian is all right with this moralist; but for a Freethinker to withhold his views from an intolerant religious world is a detestable crime.

As a biographer of Lincoln, Holland possessed many advantages over Lamon. His work was written and published immediately after the awful tragedy, when almost the entire reading public was deeply interested in everything that pertained to Lincoln's life. So far as Lincoln's religious views are concerned, he advocated the popular side of the question; for while those outside of the church cared but little about the matter, the church desired the influence of his great name, and was ready to reward those who assisted her in obtaining it. Holland, too, had an established reputation as an author – had nearly as large a class of readers as any writer in this country. His name alone was sufficient to guarantee a large circulation to any book he might produce. Lamon, on the other hand, possessed but a single advantage over his rival, that of having the truth on his side. And while "truth is mighty," and will in the end prevail, yet how often is it "crushed to earth" and for the time obscured. In view of all this, it is not strange that the public should be so slow to reject the fictions of Holland and accept the facts of Lamon.

That Lamon's *Life of Lincoln* is wholly undeserving of adverse criticism, is not claimed. He has, perhaps, given undue prominence to some matters connected with Lincoln's private affairs which might with propriety have been consigned to oblivion. A larger manifestation of charity, too, for the imperfections of those with whom Lincoln mingled, especially in the humbler walks of life, would not have detracted from its merit. And yet, those who desire to know Lincoln as he really was, should read Lamon rather than Holland. In Lamon's work, Lincoln's character is a rugged oak, towering above its fellows and clothed in nature's livery; in Holland's work, it is a dead tree with the bark taken off, the knots planed down, and varnished.

In the *New York World* appeared the following just estimate of these two biographies:

Mr. Ward H. Lamon is the author of one *Life of Lin-*

coln, and Dr. J.G. Holland is the author of another. Mr. Lamon was the intimate personal and political friend of Mr. Lincoln, trusting and trusted, from the time of their joint practice in the Illinois Quarter Sessions to the moment of Mr. Lincoln's death at Washington. Dr. Holland was nothing to Mr. Lincoln – neither known nor knowing. Dr. Holland rushed his *Life* from the press before the disfigured corpse was fairly out of sight, while the public mind lingered with horror over the details of the tragedy, and, excited by morbid curiosity, was willing to pay for its gratification. Mr. Lamon waited many years, until all adventitious interest had subsided, and then with incredible labor and pains, produced a volume founded upon materials which for their fulness, variety, and seeming authenticity are unrivaled in the history of biographies. Dr. Holland's single volume professed to cover the whole of Mr. Lincoln's career. Mr. Lamon's single volume was modestly confined to a part of it. Dr. Holland's was an easy, graceful, off-hand performance, having but the one slight demerit of being in all essential particulars untrue from beginning to end. Mr. Lamon's was a labored, cautious, and carefully verified narrative which seems to have been accepted by disinterested critics as entirely authentic.

Dr. Holland would probably be very much shocked if anybody should ask him to bear false witness in favor of his neighbor in a court of justice, but he takes up his pen to make a record which he hopes and intends shall endure forever, and in that record deliberately bears false witness in favor of a public man whom he happened to admire, with no kind of offense to his serene and "cultured" conscience. If this were all – if Dr. Holland merely asserted his own right to compose and publish elaborate fictions on historical subjects – we might comfort ourselves with the reflection that such literature is likely to be as evanescent as it is dishonest, and let him pass in silence. But this is not all. He maintains that it is everybody's duty to help him to deceive the public and to write down his more conscientious competitor. He turns up the nose of "culture" and curls the lip of "art" at Mr. Lamon's homely narrative of facts, and gravely insists that all other noses and all other lips shall be turned up and curled because his are. He implores the public, which he insulted and gulled with his own book, to damn Mr. Lamon's, and he puts his request on the very ground that Mr. Lamon has stupidly gone and narrated undeniable truths, whereby he has demolished an empty shrine that was profitable to many, and broken a painted idol that might have served for a god.

The names of Holland and Lamon are not of themselves and by themselves illustrious; but starting from the title-pages of the two *Lives of Lincoln*, and representing, as they do, the two schools of biography writers, the one stands for a principle and the other for the want of it.

CHAPTER EIGHT:
Testimony of Hon. John T. Stuart and Col. James H. Matheny

☆　☆　☆　☆

Testimony of Hon. John P. Stuart – Testimony of Col. James H.
Matheny – Stuart's Disclaimer – Matheny's Disclaimer
Examination and Authorship of Disclaimers,
Including the Edwards and Lewis Letters

Besides his own testimony concerning Lincoln's unbelief, Colonel Lamon cites the testimony of ten additional witnesses: Hon. Wm. H. Herndon, Hon. John T. Stuart, Col. James H. Matheny, Dr. C.H. Ray, Wm. H. Hannah, Esq., Mr. Jas. W. Keys, Hon. Jesse W. Fell, Col. John G. Nicolay, Hon. David Davis and Mrs. Mary Lincoln. The testimony of Mr. Herndon having already been presented, the testimony of Mr. Stuart and Colonel Matheny will next be given. This testimony was procured by Mr. Herndon for the purpose of refuting the erroneous statements of Dr. Holland.

Hon. John T. Stuart who was for a time a member of Congress from Illinois, was the first law partner of Lincoln. He says:

> Lincoln went further against Christian beliefs and doctrines and principles than any man I ever heard: he shocked me. I don't remember the exact line of his argument – I suppose it was against the inherent defects, so called, of the Bible, and on grounds of reason. Lincoln always denied that Jesus was the Christ of God – denied that Jesus was the son of God, as understood and maintained by the Christian church. The Rev. Dr. Smith, who

wrote a letter, tried to convert Lincoln from Infidelity so late as 1858, and couldn't do it.[1]

Col. James H. Matheny was one of Lincoln's most intimate friends, and was for many years his chief political manager. He testifies as follows:

> I knew Mr. Lincoln as early as 1834-7; know he was an Infidel. He and W. D. Herndon used to talk Infidelity in the Clerk's office in this city, about the years 1837-40. Lincoln attacked the Bible and the New Testament on two grounds: first, from the inherent or apparent contradictions under its lids; second, from the grounds of reason. Sometimes he ridiculed the Bible and the New Testament, sometimes seemed to scoff it, though I shall not use that word in its full and literal sense. I never heard that Lincoln changed his views, though his personal and political friend from 1834 to 1860. Sometimes Lincoln bordered on Atheism. He went far that way and shocked me. I was then a young man, and believed what my good mother told me. Stuart and Lincoln's office was in what is called Hoffman's Row, on North Fifth street, near the public square. It was in the same building as the Clerk's office, and on the same floor. Lincoln would come into the Clerk's office, where I and some young men – Evan Butler, Newton Francis and others – were writing or staying, and would bring the Bible with him; would read a chapter, argue against it. Lincoln then had a smattering of geology, if I recollect it. Lincoln often, if not wholly, was an Atheist; at least, bordered on it. Lincoln was enthusiastic in his Infidelity. As he grew older, he grew more discreet, didn't talk much before strangers about his religion; but to friends, close and bosom ones, he was always open and avowed, fair and honest; but to strangers, he held them off from policy. Lincoln used to quote Burns. Burns helped Lincoln to be an Infidel, as I think; at least he found in Burns a like thinker and feeler.
>
> From what I know of Mr. Lincoln and his views of Christianity, and from what I know as honest, well-founded rumor; from what I have heard his best friends say and regret for years;

---

1. Lamon's *Life of Lincoln*, p. 488.

from what he never denied when accused, and from what Lincoln has hinted and intimated, to say no more, he did write a little book on Infidelity, at or near New Salem, in Menard county, about the year 1834 or 1835. 1 have stated these things to you often. Judge Logan, John T. Stuart, yourself, know what I know, and some of you more.

Mr. Herndon, you insist on knowing something which you know I possess, and got as a secret, and that is, about Lincoln's little book on Infidelity. Mr. Lincoln *did* tell me that he *did write a little book on Infidelity*. This statement I have avoided heretofore; but, as you strongly insist upon it – probably to defend yourself against charges of misrepresentations – I give it to you as I got it from Lincoln's mouth.[1]

The evidence of Stuart and Matheny, as recorded in Lamon's work, having been presented, it is now proper to state that this evidence has, in a measure, been repudiated by them. Dr. Reed, in his lecture, produced letters from them disclaiming in part or modifying the statements imputed to them. Dr. Reed says: "I have been amazed to find that the principal persons whose testimony is given in this book to prove that their old friend lived and died an Infidel, never wrote a word of it, and never gave it as their opinion or allowed it to be published as covering their estimate of Mr. Lincoln's life and religious views." Alluding to Stuart's evidence, he says: "Mr. Lamon has attributed to Mr. Stuart testimony the most disparaging and damaging to Mr. Lincoln's character and opinions – testimony with Mr. Stuart utterly repudiates, both as to language and sentiment." Regarding Matheny's testimony, he says: "Mr. Matheny testifies that he never wrote a word of what is attributed to him; that it is not a fair representation of either his language or his opinions, and that he never would have allowed such an article to be published as covering his estimate of Mr. Lincoln's life and character."

The following is the disclaimer of Mr. Stuart:

---

1. *Ibid.*, pp. 487, 488.

Springfield, Dec. 17th, 1872.

Rev. J. A. Reed:

Dear Sir —

My attention has been called to a statement in relation to the religious opinions of Mr. Lincoln, purporting to have been made by me, and published in Lamon's *Life of Lincoln*. The language of that statement is not mine; it was not written by me, and I did not see it until it was in print. I was once interviewed on the subject of Mr. Lincoln's religious opinions, and doubtless said that Mr. Lincoln was in the earlier part of his life an Infidel. I could not have said that Dr. Smith tried to convert Lincoln from Infidelity so late as 1858, and couldn't do it. In relation to that point I stated, in the same conversation, some facts which are omitted in that statement, and which I will briefly repeat. That Eddie, a child of Mr. Lincoln, died in 1848 or 1849, and that he and his wife were in deep grief on the account. That Dr. Smith, then pastor of the First Presbyterian church of Springfield, at the suggestion of a lady friend of theirs, called upon Mr. and Mrs. Lincoln, and that first visit resulted, in great intimacy and friendship between them, lasting till the death of Mr. Lincoln, and continuing with Mrs. Lincoln till the death of Dr. Smith. I stated that I had heard at the time that Dr. Smith and Mr. Lincoln had much discussion in relation to the truth of the Christian religion, and that Dr. Smith had furnished Mr. Lincoln with books to read on that subject, and among others one which had been written by himself, sometime previous, on Infidelity; and that Dr. Smith claimed that after this investigation Mr. Lincoln had changed his opinions, and became a believer in the truth of the Christian religion; that Mr. Lincoln and myself never conversed upon that subject, and I had no personal knowledge as to his alleged change of opinion. I stated, however, that it was certainly true that up to that time Mr. Lincoln had never regularly attended any place of religious worship, but that after that time he rented a pew in the First Presbyterian church, and with his family constantly attended the worship in that church until he went to Washington as President. This much I said at the time, and I can now add that the Hon. Ninian W. Edwards, the brother-in-law of Mr. Lincoln, has, within a few days, informed me that when Mr. Lincoln commenced attending the First Presbyterian church he admitted to him that his views had undergone the change claimed by Dr. Smith. I would further say that Dr. Smith was a man of great ability, and on theological and metaphysical subjects had few superiors and not many equals. Truthfulness was a prominent trait in Mr. Lincoln's character, and it would be impossible for any intimate friend of his to believe that he ever aimed to deceive, either by his words or his conduct.

Yours truly,
John T. Stuart

Col. Matheny's disclaimer is as follows:

Springfield, Dec. 16th, 1872.

Rev. J.A. Reed:

 Dear Sir —

 The language attributed to me in Lamon's book is not from my pen. I did not write it, and it does not express my sentiments of Mr. Lincoln's entire life and character. It is a mere collection of sayings gathered from private conversations that were only true of Mr. Lincoln's earlier life. I would not have allowed such an article to be printed over my signature as covering my opinion of Mr. Lincoln's life and religious sentiments. While I do believe Mr. Lincoln to have been an Infidel in his former life, when his mind was as yet unformed, and his associations principally with rough and skeptical men, yet I believe he was a very different man in later life, and that after associating with a different class of men and investigating the subject, he was a firm believer in the Christian religion.

Yours truly,
Jas. H. Matheny.

This disclosure startles you, my dear reader. But be patient. I will show you that this apparently mortal thrust of Dr. Reed's was made, not with a lance, but with a boomerang.

When Reed made his assault upon Lamon's witnesses, all stood firm but two — two old Springfield politicians whose political aspirations had not yet become extinct — John T. Stuart and James H. Matheny. These men had been among the first to testify in regard to Lincoln's unbelief. His Christian biographers had misrepresented his religious views; they believed that the fraud ought to be exposed, and they were ready and willing to aid in the work. Their testimony exhibits a frankness that is truly commendable. They knew that lying was a vice, but they did not know that truth-telling was a crime. They had yet to learn that the church tolerates murder more readily than the promulgation of a truth that is antagonistic to her creed. But this fact they were destined to learn. Lamon's work had scarcely been issued from the press before he was anathematized and his book proscribed. The merciless attack that had already been commenced upon Herndon portended danger to them. Nor had they long to wait. In December, 1872, they were approached by Reed and his coadjutors. They were informed that the idol which their ruthless iconoclasm had helped to break must be repaired. They were given to understand that if they repented of the part they had performed and recanted, peace would be their portion here and endless bliss hereafter; but that if they did not, endless misery would begin on Jan. 1, A.D. 1873.

The situation was critical. They did not like to tell the world that they had borne false witness against the dead, nor did they, any more than Galileo, wish to wear a martyr's crown. A compromise was finally effected. It was incidentally ascertained by Reed that their evidence as presented by Lamon was not originally given in the shape of a letter or a written statement, but orally. A happy thought suggested itself − one worthy of the unscrupulous theological pettifogger that he is. The thought was this: "Say to the public, or rather let me say it for you, that you did not *write* a word of the testimony attributed to you." Just as a witness in court might point to the stenographer's report of his testimony and say, "I did not write a word of that."

In addition to this, Mr. Stuart, in endeavoring to explain away, as far as possible, the obnoxious character of his testimony, declared that some things which he did say at the time his testimony was given had been omitted; while something he did not say was inserted. They were both trivial matters, hardly worthy of notice, even if true, and having no especial bearing upon the case. But they served an admirable purpose in enabling Reed to say that the testimony adduced by Lamon was "abridged and distorted."

Stuart's disclaimer, then, divested of its misleading verbiage, contains but two points. In the first place, he says: "I could not have said that 'Dr. Smith tried to convert Lincoln from Infidelity so late as 1858, and couldn't do it.'" This sentence, like everything else in these disclaimers, is cunningly worded and intended to deceive. One would naturally suppose the idea he intends to convey is that he never declared that Dr. Smith tried to convert Lincoln and couldn't do it. This, it has been ascertained, is not his meaning. What he means is this: "I could not have said that 'Dr. Smith tried to convert Lincoln from Infidelity, *so late as* 1858, and couldn't do it.'" His denial is a mere quibble about a date. He did undoubtedly say just what he is reported to have said. But admitting a doubt, and giving him the benefit of this doubt, by throwing out the disputed date, the passage is not less damaging than it was before: "Dr. Smith tried to convert Lincoln from Infidelity, and couldn't do it." But let us omit the entire sentence, and the testimony of Mr. Stuart that remains, about which there is no dispute, that portion of his testimony which he admits to be correct – is as follows:

> Lincoln went further against Christian beliefs and doctrines and principles than any man I ever heard; he shocked me. I don't remember the exact line of his argument; suppose it was against the inherent defects, so called, of the Bible, and on grounds of reason. Lincoln always denied that Jesus was the Christ of God – denied that Jesus was the Son of God, as understood and maintained by the Christian church.

In the second place, Mr. Stuart complains that the rumors concerning Dr. Smith's attempted conversion of Lincoln which he had mentioned to Mr. Herndon at the time of giving his testimony, were omitted. They were, and very properly, too. Mr. Stuart, or any other good lawyer, would have omitted them. Mr. Herndon desired him to testify about what he *knew,* and not about what he had *heard,* especially as he was going to headquarters in regard to these rumors. He wrote to Dr. Smith himself about them, received his testimony, and gave it to the public.

Stuart affects to believe that this story, which Ninian Edwards is dragged around by Reed to verify, may possibly have been true. But in the same sentence, he refutes this idea, and refutes the claim itself, by saying: "I had no personal knowledge as to his alleged change of opinion." Stuart was a family connection of Lincoln, and if Lincoln had been converted, he, as well as every other person in Springfield, would have known it.

He states that Dr. Smith's first visit to Lincoln was "at the suggestion of a lady friend." To have avoided another glaring contradiction in the evidence of his witnesses, Reed should have had Major Stuart state that this "lady friend" was Thomas Lewis. As it is, the account given by Stuart of Dr. Smith's first visit and acquaintance with Lincoln is entirely at variance with the account given by Mr. Lewis in his letter, quoted in Chapter One.

Mr. Stuart evidently entertained no very kind opinion of Colonel Lamon's work, and this made him all the more disposed to accede to Reed's demands. His position on the slavery question, for a time, was one which, in the light of subsequent events, he had no reason to be proud of, and Lamon in narrating the acts of Lincoln's life found it necessary frequently to refer to this. Such passages as the following were calculated not only to make him offended at Lamon, but jealous of Herndon:

> Mr. Lincoln was beset by warm friends and by old coadjutors, and besought to pause in his anti-slavery course while there was yet time. Among these there was none more earnest or persuasive than John T. Stuart, who was but the type of a class. . . . But Mr. Herndon was more than a match for the full array against him. An earnest man, instant in season and out of season, he spoke with the eloquence of apparent truth and of real personal love. . . .
>
> John T. Stuart was keeping his eye on Lincoln, with the view of keeping him on his side – the totally dead conservative side.[2]

Colonel Matheny was not prepared to deny the correct-

---

2. *Ibid.*, pp. 352, 374.

ness of a single statement in his testimony, but was forced to modify its bearing as a whole. He was made to say: "It does not express my sentiments of Mr. Lincoln's entire life and character." Now, anyone who reads his evidence cannot fail to observe that he did intend to cover Lincoln's entire life and character. There is not in it the slightest intimation that he referred merely to a part of his life. Indeed, there is one statement in his evidence which utterly precludes such an assumption. He expressly says: "I never heard that Lincoln changed his views, though his personal and political friend from 1834 to 1860." But Reed must have a sufficient portion of his life reserved in which to inject the story of his alleged conversion; and so Matheny's offense was condoned on the condition that he retain the earlier part of Lincoln's life for his testimony to rest upon, and concede the remainder to Reed for "The Later Life and Religious Sentiments of Lincoln." This division of Lincoln's life is quite indefinite, but Reed would have us believe that Colonel Matheny's evidence relates wholly to that portion of his life anterior to 1848, when Dr. Smith began the task of Christianizing him. Matheny's disclaimer is dated Dec. 16, 1872. On Dec. 9, 1873, he made the following explanation, which was published in a Springfield paper:

> What I mean, in my Reed letter, by Mr. Lincoln's earlier life, is his whole life and history in Illinois. In Illinois, and up to the time he left for Washington, he was, as I understand it, a confirmed Infidel. What I mean by Mr. Lincoln's later life, is his Washington life, where he associated with religious people, when and where I believe he thought he became a Christian. I told Mr. Reed all this just before signing the letter spoken of. I knew nothing of Mr. Lincoln's investigation into the subject of Christianity.

He says that his evidence "is a mere collection of sayings gathered from private conversations." It is doubtless true that he had many private conversations with Mr. Herndon on this subject; but his published testimony was all given at one sitting, and more, *he signed that testimony.* Every word attributed to him in Lamon's work, and repeated in this chapter, originally appeared above his signature.

The concluding words of his disclaimer are as follows:

> While I do believe Mr. Lincoln to have been an Infidel in his former life, when his mind was as yet unformed, and his associations principally with rough and skeptical men, yet I believe he was a very different man in later life; and that after associating with a different class of men, and investigating the subject, he was a firm believer in the Christian religion.

These words, as modified by the following, constitute a most remarkable statement: "In Illinois, and up to the time he left for Washington, he was, as I understand it, a confirmed Infidel. What I mean by Mr. Lincoln's later life, is his Washington life, where he associated with religious people."

Colonel Matheny confines Lincoln's Infidelity to that portion of his life "when his mind was as yet unformed," and affirms that this portion comprised all the years preceding his removal to Washington in 1861. Thus during the first fifty-two years of Lincoln's life, "his mind was as yet unformed." His enviable reputation as one of the foremost lawyers of Illinois was achieved while "his mind was as yet unformed;" when his friends sent him to Congress, "his mind was as yet unformed;" when he made his Bloomington speech, "his mind was as yet unformed;" when he delivered his famous Springfield speech," his mind was as yet unformed;" when he conducted his masterly debates with Stephen A. Douglas, "his mind was as yet unformed;" when he prepared and delivered that model of political addresses, the Cooper Institute address, "his mind was as yet unformed;" when at the Chicago Convention he outstripped in the race for Presidential nominee such eminent leaders as Seward and Chase, "his mind was as yet unformed;" when he was elected Chief Magistrate of this great nation, "his mind was as yet unformed."

It was only by leaving Illinois and going to Washington that he was thrown into religious society. Washington politicians are noted for their piety, you know. According to Matheny, *et al.*,

New Salem was a second Sodom, Springfield a second Gomorrah and Washington a sort of New Jerusalem, inhabited chiefly by saints.

Neither in Matheny's letter, nor in his interpretation of this letter, is there a word to indicate that he recognized the fact that Lincoln went to Washington to assume the office and perform the duties of President. On the contrary, the whole tenor of his remarks is to the effect that he believed the people sent him there on account of his wickedness, and while "his mind was as yet unformed," to attend a reform school, and that subsequently he entered a theological seminary, and there died.

The most amusing feature of Matheny's letter is that he unwittingly certifies that his own character was not good. He declares that Lincoln was an Infidel because his associations were "with rough and skeptical men;" but that after removing to Washington and "associating with a different class of men," he became a Christian. Now, it is well known that one of the most conspicuous of his "rough and skeptical" associates in Illinois was James H. Matheny.

Colonel Matheny, in his explanatory remarks, says: "I *believe* he *thought* he became a Christian;" and in almost the next breath says, "I knew nothing of Mr. Lincoln's investigation into the subject of Christianity." Can anything be more unreasonable than this? Colonel Matheny knowing that Lincoln was a confirmed Infidel – an Infidel when he went to Washington – knowing nothing about his having afterward investigated Christianity – knowing that he had no time for such an investigation, and yet believing that Lincoln thought he became a Christian! Why did he not mention this when he gave his testimony? The fact is, he did not believe that Lincoln became a Christian; but with an orthodox club raised above his head, he found it very convenient to *profess* to believe it.

As Mr. Reed has endeavored to prove that Lamon and Herndon did not faithfully report the evidence of Stuart and Matheny, it is but just that Mr. Herndon, who took down their testimony, be permitted to speak in his own defense. In his Springfield lecture, delivered in Major Stuart's town, if not in his presence, referring to Stuart's testimony, he says:

> Mr. Stuart did not write the note and no one ever said he did. What is there stated was the substance of a conversation between Mr. Stuart and myself about Mr. Lincoln's religion. I took down in a note in his office and in his presence his words and ideas as I did in other cases. The conversation spoken of took place in Mr. Stuart's office, and in the east room. Mr. Stuart does not deny that the note is substantially correct. He simply says he could not have said that Dr. Smith tried to convert Mr. Lincoln, and couldn't do it. I well remember that he did use this language. It seemed to do him good to say it. . . . It seems that Mr. Stuart had heard that Mr. Lincoln and Dr. Smith had much discussion about Christianity, but he failed to hear of Mr. Lincoln's conversion, or anything like it, and well might he say, *as he did,* that "Dr. Smith tried to convert Mr. Lincoln, *but couldn't do it.*"

Any charitably disposed person, knowing the general good character of both men, instead of crying "Fraud!" as Reed has done, will readily conclude that Mr. Herndon was mistaken, or that Mr. Stuart had forgotten just what he did say, and is it not more reasonable to suppose that the latter gentleman, in the lapse of six years, should have forgotten some things he said, than that Mr. Herndon, who recorded them the moment they were uttered, should be mistaken?

Alluding to Colonel Matheny's evidence, in the same lecture, Mr. Herndon says:

> The next gentleman introduced by Mr. Reed is Col. James H. Matheny. He is made to say, in a letter addressed to Mr. Reed, that he did not write the statement in Lamon's *Life of Lincoln.* I do not claim that he did. I wrote it in the court house – this hall – in Mr. Matheny's presence, and at his dictation. I read it over to him and he approved it. I wrote it all at once as he spoke it to me; it is not made up of scraps – "a mere collection of sayings gathered from private conversations, that were only true of Mr. Lincoln's earlier life." I say that this statement was written all at one time and place, and not at different times and places. Let any critic, any man of common

sense, read it and he will say: "This was all written at once." I appeal to the manner – the close connection of words and ideas in which it runs – word with word, sentence with sentence, and idea with idea, for the proof that it was made at one sitting. Mr. Matheny has often told me that Mr. Lincoln was an Infidel. He admits this in his letter to Mr. Reed. He never intimated in that or any other conversation with me that he believed that Mr. Lincoln in his later life became a Christian.

In a letter dated Sept. 14, 1887, Mr. Herndon writes: "I acted in this matter honestly, and I will always abide by my notes taken down at the time. I was cautious – very careful of what I did, because I knew that the church would damn me and prove me false if it could. I stood on the exactness of truth squarely."

I have thus far assumed that Stuart and Matheny really wrote the letters of disclaimer addressed to Reed. Mr. Reed states that he is "amazed to find" that they did not write the statements attributed to them by Lamon. The reader is by this time sufficiently familiar with this reverend gentleman's methods that he will *not* be "amazed to find" that Stuart and Matheny did not write these disclaimers. I now affirm that James H. Matheny did not write a word of the letter purporting to have been written by him. *It was written by the Rev. J. A. Reed!* We have not the expressed declaration of Mr. Stuart that this is true of the letter imputed to him, but there is other evidence which makes it clearly apparent that this letter was also written by Mr. Reed.

Nor is this all. I shall now endeavor to show that the greater part of the evidence presented by Reed, in his lecture, was composed and written by himself. Let us take the four letters credited respectively to Edwards, Lewis, Stuart, and Matheny. I shall attempt to demonstrate the common origin of these letters – first, by their form; secondly, by the language of their contents.

The different forms employed in epistolary correspondence are numerous, far more numerous than generally supposed. To illustrate: four hundred letters, written by as many different persons, and all addressed to the same person, were, without examination, divided into one hundred parcels of four letters each. They were then examined in regard to the form employed by the writer. The heading, the address, the introduction, and the subscription were noted – no attention being paid to the body of the letter, or the signature. In not one of these one hundred parcels were found four letters having the same form. The heading of these letters exhibited nine different forms; the address, fourteen; the introduction, eight; and the subscription, eleven.

Again, nearly every writer employs certain idioms of language that are peculiar to him, and which reveal his identity, even though he tries to conceal it.

Let us now institute a brief analysis of the four letters under consideration. Errors will be noticed, not for the purpose of reflecting upon the literary attainments of the writer, but solely with a view of discovering his identity. These are mostly of a trivial character, confined to marks of punctuation, etc.; and it is a recognized fact that a majority of educated persons, including many professional writers, are more or less deficient in the art of punctuation. In proof of the common authorship of these four letters, the following reasons are submitted:

1. In all of them we recognize a stiff formality – a studied effort to conform to one ideal standard.

2. All of them were written at Springfield, Ill., and all omit the name of the State.

3. In each of them, the day of the month is followed by the suffix "th." This, if not wholly improper, is not common usage. Had these letters been written by the four persons to whom they are ascribed, at least three of them would have omitted it.

4. In all, but one, the address is "Rev. J.A. Reed," and in the exception the writer merely substitutes "Jas." for "J."

5. In each of them the address is followed by a colon instead of a comma, the proper mark to use. Had they been written by four persons, it is possible that a part, or even all, would have made an error, but it is highly improbable that all would have made the *same* error.

6. In these letters, the introductory words are uniformly "Dear Sir" – the most common form of introduction, and the one that a writer, in drafting a letter addressed to himself, would most

naturally employ.

7. In every instance, the introduction is followed by a dash instead of a colon – a uniformity of error, again.

8. In the subscription, the term, "Yours truly," is invariably used, except in the Lewis letter, which concludes with "Yours, etc."

9. The Edwards letter and the Lewis letter begin with the same idea, expressed in nearly the same words. Edwards is made to say, "A short time after the Rev. Dr. Smith," etc.; and Lewis, "Not long after Dr. Smith."

10. Omitting the introductory sentence in the Stuart letter, which is merely the expansion of an idea used in writing the Matheny letter on the preceding day, the Stuart and Matheny letters begin with the same idea. Stuart says: "The language of that statement is not mine; it was not written by me." Matheny says: "The language attributed to me . . . is not from my pen. I did not write it." Reed himself uses substantially the same language that is ascribed to them. Had their statements, as published in Lamon's work, been forgeries, or grossly inaccurate, they might have used the language quoted above. Under the circumstances they would not have used it. Major Stuart and Colonel Matheny were lawyers, not pettifoggers.

11. These prefatory sentences of Stuart and Matheny both begin with the same words – "the language."

12. In both the Edwards and Lewis letters, reference is made to a theological work which Dr. Smith is said to have written. The writer of neither letter is able to state the name of the book; Dr. Reed is unable to state the name of it; Dr. Smith himself does not mention the name of it; but he does plainly state that it was a work on the Bible. For "the business he had on hand," however, it suited Reed's purpose better to give a semi-erroneous impression of its character, and so he affirms that it was a work on "the evidences of Christianity." Curiously enough, in the Edwards letter and again in the Lewis letter, the book is described as a work on "the evidences of Christianity."

13. The Edwards letter reports Lincoln as saying: "I have been reading *a work of Dr. Smith on the evidences of Christian-*

ity." The Lewis letter represents him as saying that "He had seen and partially read *a work of Dr. Smith on the evidences of Christianity.*" Here are ten consecutive words in the two letters identical.

14. Mr. Reed, in his lecture, never once uses the word "Christianity," except as above noticed to describe Dr. Smith's book; he always uses the words "the Christian religion" – employing this term no less than seven times. This usage is not common. An examination of various theological writings shows that "Christianity" is used twenty times where "the Christian religion" is used once. Yet in these letters the word "Christianity" is not to be found, except in the same sense as used by Dr. Reed, while "the Christian religion" occurs in each of the four letters.

15. "The truth of the Christian religion" is a favorite phrase with Reed, occurring three times in his lecture. This phrase also occurs three times in these letters – once in the Edwards letter, and twice in the Stuart letter.

16. Reed has much to say about Lincoln's "life and religious sentiments;" in fact, his lecture is entitled, "The Later Life and Religious Sentiments of Abraham Lincoln." In the Matheny letter, too, we find "Mr. Lincoln's life and religious sentiments."

17. The words "earlier" and "later" are frequently used by Reed in connection with Lincoln's life. The same words are used in the Stuart and Matheny letters, and in the same connection.

18. The Stuart letter is, for the most part, devoted to the narration of "some facts" which Mr. Stuart is said to have presented to Mr. Herndon, beginning with this: "That Eddie, a child of Mr. Lincoln, died in 1848 or 1849," etc. Now, Mr. Stuart well knew that, during all this time, Mr. Herndon was the intimate associate of Lincoln and thoroughly familiar with every event in his history. The "facts" given in this letter are not such as Mr. Stuart would have communicated to Mr. Herndon, but they are such as Mr. Reed would naturally desire to place before the public.

19. Nothing in Dr. Reed's career has excited his vanity more than the fact that he was pastor of the First Presbyterian Church of Springfield – the church which Lincoln once attended.

Consequently, the "First Presbyterian Church" is a conspicuous object in his lecture, and nowhere is it more conspicuous than in these letters. In the Stuart letter it appears three times, and the writer never fails to state that it was the *"First* Presbyterian Church" – the church of which Dr. Reed was pastor.

20. According to the principle of accretion, if two articles or letters are written on the same subject, the second will usually be longer than the first. This is true of these letters. The Lewis letter, relating to Smith's reputed conversion of Lincoln, was written after the Edwards letter relative to the same subject, and is longer. The Stuart disclaimer, which is the longer of the two, was written after the Matheny disclaimer.

From the foregoing, is it not clearly evident that these four letters were all written by the same person? If so, then knowing that Dr. Reed wrote one of them – the Matheny letter – does it not necessarily follow that he wrote them all?

In the Gurley testimony, such expressions as "the Christian religion" and "the truth of the Christian religion," together with the Reed story concerning Lincoln's intention of making a profession of religion, reveal the authorship of this testimony also.

CHAPTER NINE:
Testimony of the Remaining Witnesses Presented by Lamon
☆ ☆ ☆ ☆

Dr. C.H. Ray – Wm. H. Hannah, Esq. – James W. Keys
Hon. Jesse W. Fell – Col. John G. Nicolay – Hon. David Davis
Mrs. Mary Lincoln – Injustice to Mrs. Lincoln – Answer to Reed's
Pretended Refutation of the Testimony of Lamon's Witnesses

Seven of Lamon's witnesses Ray, Hannah, Keys, Fell, Nicolay, Davis, and Mrs. Lincoln remain to testify. The testimony of these witnesses will now be presented.

Dr. C.H. Ray

Dr. Ray, editor of the *Chicago Tribune,* a prominent figure in Illinois .politics thirty years ago, and a personal friend and admirer of Lincoln, testifies as follows:

> You knew Mr. Lincoln far better than I did, though I knew him well; and you have served up his leading characteristics in a way that I should despair of doing, if I should try. I have only one thing to ask: that you do not give Calvinistic theology a chance to claim him as one of its saints and martyrs. He went to the Old School Church; but, in spite of that outward assent to the horrible dogmas of the sect, I have reason from himself to know that his vital purity, if that means belief in the impossible, was of a negative sort.[1]

---

1. Lamon's *Life of Lincoln*, pp. 489, 490.

Dr. Ray states that Lincoln held substantially the same theological opinions as those held by Theodore Parker.

William H. Hannah

A leading member of the Bloomington bar, when Lincoln practiced there, was Wm. H. Hannah. He was an honest, truthful man, and knew Lincoln well. Concerning Lincoln's views on the doctrine of endless punishment, Mr. Hannah says: "Since 1856 Mr. Lincoln told me that he was a kind of immortalist; but that he never could bring himself to believe in eternal punishment; that man lived but a little while here, and that, if eternal punishment were man's doom, he should spend that little life in vigilant and ceaseless preparation by never-ending prayer."[2]

James W. Keys

Mr. Jas. W. Keys, an old and respected citizen of Springfield, who became acquainted with Lincoln soon after his removal there, and who had many conversations with him on the subject of theology, says: "As to the Christian theory, that Christ is God, or equal to the Creator, he said that it had better be taken for granted; for, by the test of reason, we might become Infidels on that subject, for evidence of Christ's divinity came to us in a somewhat doubtful shape."[3]

Hon. Jesse W. Fell

Jesse W. Fell, who died at Bloomington in the spring of 1887, was one of the best known, and most highly respected citizens of Illinois. He was Secretary of the Republican State Central Committee during the memorable Lincoln-Douglas campaign, and was largely instrumental in bringing Lincoln forward as a candidate for the Presidency in 1860. It was for him that Lincoln wrote an

---

2. *Life of Lincoln*, p. 489.
3. *Ibid.*, p. 490.

autobiographical sketch of his life, which formed the basis of his campaign biographies, the *facsimile* of which appears in Lamon's *Life of Lincoln*, and in the *Lincoln Memorial Album*. Mr. Fell was a Christian of the Unitarian denomination, and there were few men for whom Lincoln had a more profound respect. The following is his testimony:

> Though everything relating to the character of this extraordinary personage is of interest, and should be fairly stated to the world, I enter upon the performance of this duty for so I regard it with some reluctance, arising from the fact that, in stating my convictions on the subject, I must necessarily place myself in opposition to quite a number who have written on this topic before me, and whose views largely pre-occupy the public mind. This latter fact, whilst contributing to my embarrassment on this subject, is, perhaps, the strongest reason, however, why the truth in this matter should be fully disclosed; and I therefore yield to your request. If there were any traits of character that stood out in bold relief in the person of Mr. Lincoln, they were those of truth and candor. He was utterly incapable of insincerity, or professing views on this or any other subject he did not entertain. Knowing such to be his true character, that insincerity, much more duplicity, were traits wholly foreign to his nature, many of his old friends were not a little surprised at finding, in some of the biographies of this great man, statements concerning his religious opinions so utterly at variance with his known sentiments. True, he may have changed or modified those sentiments after his removal from among us, though this is hardly reconcilable with the history of the man, and his entire devotion to public matters during his four years' residence at the national capital. It is possible, however, that this may be the proper solution of this conflict of opinions; or, it may be, that, with no intention on the part of anyone to mislead the public mind, those who have represented him as believing in the popular theological views of the times may have misapprehended him, as experience shows to be quite common where no special effort has been made to attain critical accuracy on a subject of this nature. This is the more probable from the well-known fact that Mr. Lincoln seldom communicated to anyone his views on this subject. But,

be this as it may, I have no hesitation whatever in saying that, whilst he held many opinions in common with the great mass of Christian believers, he did not believe in what are regarded as the orthodox or evangelical views of Christianity.

On the innate depravity of man, the character and office of the great head of the church, the atonement, the infallibility of the written revelation, the performance of miracles, the nature and design of present and future rewards and punishments (as they are popularly called) and many other subjects, he held opinions utterly at variance with what are usually taught in the church. I should say that his expressed views on these and kindred topics were such as, in the estimation of most believers, would place him entirely outside the Christian pale. Yet, to my mind, such was not the true position, since his principles and practices and the spirit of his whole life were of the very kind we universally agree to call Christian; and I think this conclusion is in no wise affected by the circumstance that he never attached himself to any religious society whatever.

His religious views were eminently practical, and are summed up, as I think, in these two propositions: the fatherhood of God, and the brotherhood of man. He fully believed in a superintending and overruling Providence that guides and controls the operations of the world, but maintained that law and order, and not their violation or suspension, are the appointed means by which this Providence is exercised.

I will not attempt any specification of either his belief or disbelief on various religious topics, as derived from conversations with him at different times during a considerable period; but, as conveying a general view of his religious or theological opinions, will state the following facts: Some eight or ten years prior to his death, in conversing with him on this subject, the writer took occasion to refer, in terms of approbation, to the sermons and writings generally of Dr. W. E. Channing; and, finding he was considerably interested in the statement I made of the opinions held by that author, I proposed to present him a copy of Channing's entire works, which I soon after did. Subsequently, the contents of these volumes, together with the writings of Theodore Parker, furnished him, as he informed me, by his friend and law-partner, Mr. Herndon, became naturally the topics of conversation with us; and though far from believing there was an entire harmony of views on his part with either of those authors, yet they were generally much admired and approved by him.

No religious views with him seemed to find any favor, except of the practical and rationalistic order; and if, from my recollections on this subject, I was called upon to designate an author whose views most nearly represented Mr. Lincoln's on this subject, I would say that author was Theodore Parker.

As you have asked from me a candid statement of my recollections on this topic, I have thus briefly given them, with the hope that they may be of some service in rightly settling a question about which as I have good reason to believe the public mind has been greatly misled. Not doubting that they will accord, substantially, with your own recollections, and that of his other intimate and confidential friends, and with the popular verdict after this matter shall have been properly canvassed, I submit them.[4]

Mr. Fell's testimony is full and explicit. He affirms that Lincoln rejected nearly all the leading tenets of orthodox Christianity; the inspiration of the Scriptures, the divinity of Christ, the innate depravity of man, the atonement, the performance of miracles, and future rewards and punishments. "His expressed views on these and kindred topics," Mr. Fell says, "were such as, in the estimation of most believers, would place him entirely outside the Christian pale." Mr. Fell, himself, was not disposed to withhold from Lincoln the appellation of Christian, but it was only because he stood upon the broad Liberal Christian, or rather non-Christian, platform which permitted him to welcome a Theist, like Parker; a Pantheist, like Emerson; or even an Agnostic, like Ingersoll.

Col. John G. Nicolay

The next witness introduced by Lamon, is Col. John G. Nicolay, Lincoln's private secretary at the White House. Nicolay's relations with the President were more intimate than those of any

---

4. *Life of Lincoln*, pp. 490-492.

other man; To quote the words of Lincoln's partner, "Mr. Lincoln loved him and trusted him." His testimony is among the most important that this controversy has elicited: It proves beyond the shadow of a doubt that all these stories concerning Lincoln's alleged 'conversation at Washington are false, that he did not change his belief, that he died as he had always lived a Freethinker. In a letter written May 27, 1865, just six weeks after Lincoln's death Colonel Nicolay says:

> Mr. Lincoln did not, to my knowledge, in any way, change his religious ideas, opinions or beliefs, from the time he left Springfield till the day of his death. I do not know just what they were, never having heard him explain them in detail, but I am very sure he gave no outward indications of his mind having undergone any change in that regard while here.[5]

Hon. David Davis

One of the most important, and in some respects the most eminent witness summoned to testify in regard to this question, is the Hon. David Davis. In moral character he stood above reproach, in intellectual ability, almost without a peer. Every step in his career was marked by unswerving integrity and freedom from prejudice. His rulings and decisions in the lower courts of Illinois, and on the bench of the Supreme Court of the United States, commanded universal respect. As a legislator, his love of truth and justice prevented him from being a political partisan. As United States Senator and Vice-President of the United States, the party that elected him could obtain his support for no measure that he deemed unjust. Referring to his acquaintance with Lincoln, Judge Davis says: "I enjoyed for over twenty years the personal friendship of Mr. Lincoln. We were admitted to the bar about the same time, and traveled for many years what is known in Illinois as the Eighth Judicial Circuit. In 1848, when I first went on the bench, the circuit embraced fourteen counties, and Mr. Lincoln went with the court to every county." A large portion of this time they passed in each

---

5. *Life of Lincoln*, p. 492.

other's company. They often rode in the, same vehicle, generally ate at the same table, and not infrequently slept together, in the same bed. The closest intimacy existed between them as long as Lincoln lived, and when he died, Mr. Davis became his executor. Judge Davis would not intentionally have misrepresented the opinions of an enemy, much less the opinions of his dear dead friend. Briefly, yet clearly, be defines the theological views of Lincoln: "He had no faith, in the Christian sense of the term had faith in laws, principles, causes, and effects philosophically."[6]

Speaking of the many stories that had been circulated concerning Lincoln's religious belief, such as the Bateman and Vinton interviews, together with the various pious speeches he is reported to have made to religious committees and delegations that visited him, such as his reputed speech to the Negroes of Baltimore, Judge Davis says: "The idea that Lincoln talked to a stranger about his religion or religious views, or made such speeches, remarks, &c., about it as are published, is to me absurd. I knew the man so well. He was the most reticent, secretive man I ever saw, or expect to see."[7]

Mrs. Mary Lincoln

But one of Lamon's witnesses remains the wife of the martyred President. Her testimony ought of itself to put this matter at rest forever. Mrs. Lincoln says: "Mr. Lincoln had no hope, and no faith, in the usual acceptation of those words."[8]

In addition to what Colonel Lamon has presented Mrs. Lincoln also stated the following: "Mr. Lincoln's maxim and philosophy were, 'What is to be, will be, and no prayers of ours can arrest the decree.' He never joined any church. He was a religious man always, I think, but was not a technical Christian."[9]

It may be charged that Mrs. Lincoln subsequently repudi-

---

6. *Life of Lincoln*, p. 489.

7. *Ibid.*

8. *Ibid.*

9. Herndon's "Religion of Lincoln."

ated a portion of this testimony. In anticipation of such a charge I will here state a few facts. This testimony was given by Mrs. Lincoln in 1865. When it was given, while her heart was pierced by the pangs of her great grief, her mind was sound. About Jan. 1, 1874, a brief article, purporting to come from her pen, appeared, in which the testimony attributed to her was in part denied. At the time this denial was written, Mrs. Lincoln had been for more than. two years insane. The chief cause in dethroning her reason was the death of her universally beloved Tad (Thomas), which occurred. on July 15, 1871. Referring to this sad event, Mr. Arnold, one of the principal witnesses on the Christian side of this controversy, says: "From this time Mrs. Lincoln, in the judgment of her most intimate friends, was never entirely responsible for her conduct."[10]

The only effect of this denial on the minds of those acquainted with the circumstances, was to excite a mingled feeling of pity and disgust pity for this unfortunate woman, and disgust for the contemptible methods of those who would take advantage of her demented condition and make her contradict the honest statements of her rational life.

Before dismissing this witness, I wish to advert to, a, subject with which many of my readers are familiar. For years, both before and after Lincoln's death, the religious press of the country was continually abusing Mrs. Lincoln. If a ball was held at the White House, she became at, once the recipient of unlimited abuse. If Lincoln attended the theater, she was accused of having dragged him there against his will. It was almost uniformly asserted that he would not have gone to the theater on that fatal night had it not been for her, and in not a few instances it was infamously hinted that she was cognizant of the plot to murder him. But even the Rev. Dr. Miner, who was acquainted with the facts, is willing to vindicate her from these imputations. He says: "It has been said that Mrs. Lincoln urged her husband to go to the theater against his will. This is not true. On the contrary, she tried to persuade him not to go."

Lincoln's biographers have, for the most part, endeavored

---

10. *Life of Lincoln*, p. 439.

to do his wife justice, and have rebuked the insults showered upon her. Alluding to President and Mrs. Lincoln, Mr. Herndon says: "All that I know ennobles both." Colonel Lamon says: "Almost ever since Mr. Lincoln's death a portion of the press has never tired of heaping brutal reproaches upon his wife and widow, whilst a certain class of his friends thought they were honoring his memory by multiplying outrages and indignities upon her at the very moment when she was broken by want and sorrow, defamed, defenseless, in the hands of thieves, and at the mercy of spies." Mr. Arnold says: "There is nothing in American history so unmanly, so devoid of every chivalric impulse as the treatment of this poor, broken-hearted woman."

The evidence of Colonel Lamon's ten witnesses has now been presented. This evidence includes, in addition to the testimony of other intimate friends, the testimony of his wife; the testimony of his first law partner, Hon. John T. Stuart; the testimony of his last law partner, Hon. Wm. H. Herndon; the testimony of his friend and political adviser, Col. James H. Matheny; the testimony of his private secretary, Col. John G. Nicolay; and the testimony of his lifelong friend and executor after death, Judge David Davis. No one can read this evidence and then honestly affirm that Abraham Lincoln was a Christian. This is the evidence, the perusal of which so thoroughly enraged that good Christian biographer, Dr. J.G. Holland; this is the evidence, the truthfulness of which the Rev. J.A. Reed, unmindful of the fate of Ananias, attempted to deny.

As a full and just answer to this attempted refutation of Lamon's witnesses by Reed, I quote from the *New York World* the following:

> This individual testimony is clear and overwhelming, without the documentary and other evidence scattered profusely through the rest of the volume. How does Mr. Reed undertake to refute it? In the first place, firstly, he pronounces it a libel, and in the second place, secondly, he is "amazed to find" and he says he has found that the principal witnesses take exception to Mr. Lamon's report of their evidence. This might have been true of many or all of Mr. Lamon's witnesses without exciting

the wonder of a rational man. Few persons, indeed, are willing to endure reproach merely for the truth's sake, and popular opinion in the Republican party of Springfield, Ill., is probably very much against Mr. Lamon. It would, therefore, be quite in the natural order if some of his witnesses who find themselves unexpectedly in print should succumb to the social and political terrorism of their place and time, and attempt to modify or explain their testimony. They zealously assisted Mr. Herndon in ascertaining the truth, and while they wanted him to tell it in full they were prudently resolved to keep their own names snugly out of sight. But Mr. Reed's statement is not true, and his amazement is entirely simulated. Two only out of the ten witnesses have gratified him by inditing, at his request, weak and guarded complaints of unfair treatment. These are John T. Stuart, a relative of the Lincolns and Edwardses, and Jim Matheny, both, of Springfield, whom Mr. Lincoln taught his peculiar doctrines, but who may by this time be deacons in Mr. Reed's church. Neither of them helps Mr. Reed's case a particle. Their epistles open, as if by concert, in form and words almost identical. They say they did not *write* the language attributed to them. The denial is wholly unnecessary, for nobody affirms that they did write it. They talked and Mr. Herndon wrote. His notes were made when the conversation occurred, and probably in their presence. At all events, they are both so conscious of the general accuracy of his report that they do not venture to deny a single word of it, but content themselves with lamenting that something else, which they did *not* say, was excluded from it. They both, however, in these very letters, repeat emphatically the material part of the statements made by them to Mr. Herndon, namely, that Mr. Lincoln was to their certain knowledge, until a very late period of his life, an 'Infidel,' and neither of them is able to tell when he ceased to be an Infidel and when he began to be a Christian. And this is all Mr. Reed makes by his re-examination of the two persons whom he is pleased to exalt as Mr. Lamon's "principal witnesses." They are but two out of the ten. What of the other eight? They have no doubt been tried and plied by Mr. Reed and his friends to no purpose; they stand fast by the record. But Mr. Reed is to be shamed neither by their speech nor their silence.

CHAPTER TEN:
Testimony of Lincoln's Relatives and Intimate Associates
☆ ☆ ☆ ☆

Mrs. Sarah Lincoln – Dennis F. Hanks – Mrs. Matilda Moore
John Hall – Wm. McNeely – Wm. G. Green – Joshua F. Speed
Green Caruthers – John Decamp – Mr. Lynan – James B. Spaulding
Ezra Stringham – Dr. G.H Ambrose – J.H. Chenery
Squire Perkins – W. Perkins – James Gorley – Dr. Wm. Jayne
Jesse K. Dubois – Hon. Joseph Gillespie – Judge Stephen T. Logan
Hon. Leonard Swett

Were I to rest my case here, the evidence already adduced is sufficient, I think, to convince any unprejudiced mind that Lincoln was not a Christian. But I do not propose to rest here. I have presented the testimony of half a score of witnesses; before I lay down my pen I shall present the testimony of nearly ten times as many more.

In this chapter will be given the testimony of some of the relatives and intimate associates of Lincoln. The testimony of his relatives confirms the claim that he was not religious in his youth; the others testify to his unbelief while a resident of New Salem and Springfield.

Mrs. Sarah Lincoln

If there was one person to whom Lincoln was more indebted than to any other, it was his stepmother, Sally Lincoln, a beautiful woman – beautiful not only in face and form, but possessed of a most lovely character. She was not highly educated, but she loved knowledge, and inspired in her step-son a love for books. She was a Christian, but she attached more importance to deed than to creed. She loved Lincoln. After his death she said: "He was dutiful to me always. I think he loved me truly. I had a son, John, who was raised with Abe. Both were good boys; but I must say, both now being dead, that Abe was the best boy I ever saw, or expect to see." Lincoln was too good and too great not to appreciate this woman's care and affection.

When the materials for Lincoln's biography were being collected, Mrs. Lincoln was considered the most reliable source from which to obtain the facts pertaining to his boyhood. Her recollections of him were recorded with the utmost care. His Christian biographers, in order to make a Sunday-school hero of him, have declared him to be a youth remarkable for his Christian piety and his love of the Bible. The statements of Mrs. Lincoln disprove this claim. The substance of her testimony, as given by Lamon, is given as follows:

> The Bible, according to Mrs. Lincoln, was not one of his studies; "he sought more congenial books." At that time he neither talked nor read upon religious subjects. If he had any opinions about them, he kept them to himself. . . .
>
> His step-mother – herself a Christian, and longing for the least sign of faith in him – could remember no circumstance that supported her hope. On the contrary, she recollected very well that he never went off into a corner, as has been said, to ponder the sacred writings, and to wet the page with his tears of penitence.[1]

Dennis F. Hanks

The next witness is Lincoln's cousin, Dennis Hanks. Mr. Hanks held "the pulpy, red, little Lincoln" in his arms before he was "twenty-four hours old," and remained his constant companion during all the years that he lived in Kentucky and Indiana. He

---

1. *Life of Lincoln*, pp. 38, 486, 487.

lived a part of the time in the Lincoln family, and married one of Lincoln's step-sisters. I met him recently at Charleston, Ill. With evident delight he rehearsed the story of Lincoln's boyhood, and reaffirmed the truthfulness of the following statements attributed to him by Lincoln's biographers:

> Abe wasn't in early life a religious man. He was a moral man strictly. . . . In after life he became more religious; but the Bible puzzled him, especially the miracles.[2]

> "Religious songs did not appear to suit him at all," says Dennis Hanks; but of profane ballads and amorous ditties he knew the words of a vast number. . . .
> Another was:

> Hail Columbia, happy land!
> If you ain't drunk, I'll be damned, –

> a song which Dennis thinks should be warbled only in the "field;" and tells us they knew and enjoyed "all such songs as this."[3]

The fitness of the above coarse travesty to be warbled, even in the fields, may well be doubted. Lamon would hardly have recorded it, and I certainly should not quote it, but for the fact that it strikingly illustrates one phase of Lincoln's "youthful piety."

Among the many Christian hymns which Lincoln parodied, Mr. Hanks recalls the following:

> How tedious and tasteless the hours.
> When I can read my title clear.
> Oh! to grace how great a debtor!
> Come, thou fount of every blessing.

---

2. *Every-Day Life of Lincoln*, p. 54.
3. Lamon's *Life of Lincoln*, pp. 58, 59.

Mrs. Matilda Moore

Mrs. Lincoln's first husband was named Johnston. By him she had three children, a son and two daughters. The latter, like their mother, developed into noble specimens of womanhood; and both loved Lincoln as tenderly, as though he had been their own brother. The elder was married to Dennis Hanks; the younger, Matilda, married Lincoln's cousin, Levi Hall, and, after his death, a gentleman named Moore.

Lamon says that Lincoln in his youth made a mockery of the popular religion; not from any lack of reverence for what he believed to be good, but because "he thought that a person had better be without it." That he was accustomed to turn so-called sacred subjects into ridicule is attested by his step-sister, Mrs. Moore. She says: "When father and mother would go to church, Abe would take down the Bible, read a verse, give out a hymn, and we would sing. Abe was about fifteen years of age. He preached and we would do the crying."[4]

John Hall

On the 28th of April, 1888, the writer, in company with Mr. Charles Biggs, of Westfield, Ill., visited the old Lincoln homestead, near Farmington, Ill. We dined with Mr. John Hall, a son of Lincoln's step-sister Matilda, in the old log-house built by Lincoln's father sixty years ago, and in which his father and step-mother died. Mr. Hall, who owns the homestead and preserves with zealous care this venerable relic, is an intelligent farmer over sixty years of age. He greatly reveres the memory of his illustrious uncle and loves to dwell on his many noble traits of character. He stated that the family tradition is that while Abe was a most honest and humane boy, he was not religious. He referred to the mock sermons he is said to have preached. "At these meetings," said Mr. Hall, "my mother would lead in the singing while Uncle Abe would lead in prayer. Among his nu-

---

4. *Every-Day Life of Lincoln*, p. 71.

merous supplications, he prayed God to put stockings on the chickens' feet in winter."

William McNeely

William McNeely, of Petersburg, Ill., who became acquainted with Lincoln in 1831, when he arrived at New Salem on a flatboat, says:

> Lincoln said he did not believe in total depravity, and although it was not popular to believe it, it was easier to do right than wrong; that the first thought was: what was right? and the second – what was wrong? Therefore it was easier to do right than wrong, and easier to take care of, as it would take care of itself. It took no effort to do wrong, and still greater effort to take care of it; but do right and it would take care of itself. . . .
> I was acquainted with him a long time, and I never knew him to do a wrong act.[5]

William G. Green

One of Lincoln's early companions at New Salem was William G. Green. He and Lincoln clerked in the same store and slept together on the same cot. The testimony of Mr. Green has not been preserved. We have simply an observation of his, incidentally made, the substance of which is thus presented by Lamon: "Lincoln's incessant reading of Shakespeare and Burns had much to do in giving to his mind the 'skeptical' tendency so fully developed by the labors of his pen in 1834-5, and in social conversations during many years of his residence at Springfield."[6]

Mr. Green's conclusion, especially in regard to Burns, is quite generally shared by Lincoln's friends. Burns's satirical poems were greatly admired by Lincoln. "Holy Willie's Prayer,"

---

5. *Lincoln Memorial Album*, pp. 393-895

6. *Life of Lincoln*, p. 145.

one of the most withering satires on orthodox Christianity ever penned, was, memorized by him. Every one of its sixteen stanzas, beginning with the following, was an Infidel shaft which he delighted to hurl at the heads of his Christian opponents:

> O thou, wha in the heavens dost dwell,
> Wha, as it pleases best thysel',
> Sends ane to heaven and ten to hell,
> A' for thy glory,
> And no for ony guid or ill
> They've done afore thee!

Joshua F. Speed

Another of Lincoln's earliest and best friends was Joshua F. Speed. When he was licensed as a lawyer and entered upon his professional career at Springfield, without a client and without a dollar, Speed assisted him to get a start. W. H. Herndon was clerking for Speed at the time, and for more than a year Lincoln, Herndon and Speed roomed together. Referring to the religious views held by Lincoln at that time, Mr. Speed, in a lecture, says: "I have often been asked what were Mr. Lincoln's religious opinions. When I knew him, in early life, he was a skeptic. He had tried hard to be a believer, but his reason could not grasp and solve the great problem of redemption as taught."

This is the testimony of an orthodox Christian, and a church-member. Mr. Speed, during the years that he was acquainted with Lincoln, was not a member of any church; but late in life he united with the Methodist church. As "the wish is father to the thought," Mr. Speed professed to believe that Lincoln before his death modified, to some extent, the radical views of his early manhood.

Green Caruthers

Soon after Lincoln removed to Springfield, he became acquainted with Mr. Green Caruthers and remained on intimate terms with him during all the subsequent years of his life. Mr.

Caruthers was a quiet, unobtrusive old gentleman, universally respected by those who knew him. The substance of his testimony is as follows: "Lincoln, Bledsoe, the metaphysician, and myself, boarded at the Globe hotel in this city. Bledsoe tended toward Christianity, if he was not a Christian. Lincoln was always throwing out his Infidelity to Bledsoe, ridiculing Christianity, and especially the divinity of Christ."

John Decamp

Another of Lincoln's most intimate Springfield friends was John Decamp. Mr. Decamp was interviewed by Mr. Herndon regarding Lincoln's religious views in July, 1887. His statement was brief, but to the point. He says: "Lincoln was an Infidel."

Mr. Lynan

In 1880, at Bismarck Grove, Kan., the writer of this delivered a lecture entitled, "Four American Infidels," a portion of which was devoted to a presentation of Lincoln's religious views. In its report of the lecture, the *Lawrence Standard,* edited by Hon. E. G. Ross, formerly United States Senator from Kansas, and more recently Governor of New Mexico, said:

> In regard to Abraham Lincoln being an Infidel, the evidence adduced was overwhelming, and was confirmed by a gentleman present, Mr. Lynan, who had known him intimately for thirty years. Mr. Lynan declared that none but personal acquaintance could enable one to realize the nobility and purity of Lincoln's character, but that he was beyond doubt or question a thorough disbeliever in the Christian scheme of salvation to the end of his life.[7]

James B. Spaulding

Mr. J.B. Spaulding, well known as one of the leading nur-

---

7. *Lawrence Standard,* Sept. 4, 1880.

serymen and horticulturists of the United States, a man of broad culture and refinement, who resides near Springfield, became intimately acquainted with Lincoln as early as 1851, and for a long time resided on the same street with him in Springfield. Mr. Spaulding says: "Lincoln perpetrated many an irreverent joke at the expense of church doctrines. Regarding the miraculous conception, he was especially sarcastic. He wrote a manuscript as radical as Ingersoll which his political friends caused to be destroyed."

Ezra Stringham

A short time since I was conversing with a party of gentlemen in Riverton, Ill. It being near Lincoln's old home, the subject of his religious belief was introduced. An old gentleman, who up to this time had not been taking part in the conversation, quietly observed: "I think I knew Lincoln's religious views about as well as any other man." "What was he?" said one of the party. "An Infidel of the first water," was the prompt response. The old gentleman was Ezra Stringham, one of Lincoln's early acquaintances in Illinois.

Dr. G. H. Ambrose

Dr. G. H. Ambrose, of Waldo, Fla., who was associated in the law business at Springfield from 1846 to 1849 with a relative of Mrs. Lincoln, says: "Mr. Lincoln was an Infidel – an outspoken one."

J. H. Chenery

Mr. J. H. Chenery, one of Springfield's pioneers – for many years owner and proprietor of the leading hotel of Springfield – says:

> Reed tried to prove that Lincoln was a church man; but everybody here knows that he was not. Once in a great while, and only once in a great while, I saw him accompany his wife

and children to church. His attacks upon the church were most bitter and sarcastic. He wrote a book against Christianity, but his friends got away with it.

Squire Perkins

A few years ago there died near Atchison, Kan., an old gentleman named Perkins. He was poor, but honest, and a bright man intellectually. He was a son of Major Perkins who was killed in the Black Hawk war. Lincoln after the fight discovered the scalp of Major Perkins, which his savage assassin had taken but lost. His first impulse was to keep it and take it home to the family of the dead soldier. Then realizing that it would only tend to intensify their grief, he opened the grave and deposited it with the body. This incident led to an intimate acquaintance between Lincoln and the younger Perkins. In June, 1880, Mr. Perkins made the following statement relative to Lincoln's religious belief:

> During all the time that I was acquainted with Abraham Lincoln I know that he was what the church calls an Infidel. I do not believe that he ever changed his opinions. When Colfax was in Atchison I had a talk with him about Lincoln. Among other things, I asked him if Lincoln had ever been converted to Christianity. He told me that he had not.

W. Perkins

Mr. Perkins, an old lawyer and journalist of Illinois, who was acquainted with Lincoln for upward of twenty years, and who was his associate counsel in several important cases, writing from Belleview, Fla., under date of August 22, 1887, says:

> . The unfair efforts that Christians have been putting forth to drag Lincoln into their waning faith betray a pitiable imbecility. Were it possible for them to get the world to believe that Washington, Jefferson, and Lincoln, all prayed, had faith, and were washed in the blood of the Lamb, would that prove the inspiration of their Bible, harmonize its contradictions, put

a ray of reason in its gross absurdities, or humanize the first one of its numerous bloody barbarities?

I knew Mr. Lincoln from the spring of 1838 till his death. Like Archibald Williams, our contemporary, an able Lord Coke lawyer, he no more believed in the inspiration of the Bible than Hume, Paine, or Ingersoll. Less inclined openly to denounce its absurdities and cruelties, or to antagonize the well-meaning credulous professors, than was Williams. Mr. Lincoln had no faith whatever in the first miracle of the Bible, or the scheme of bloody redemption it teaches. To attribute such sentiments to him, is to tarnish his well-earned reputation for common sense, and to impair the estimation of his countrymen and the world of his high sense of humanity, justice, and honor.

Two of my Presbyterian friends at Indian Point, near Petersburg, told me that they had interviewed Mr. Lincoln to prevent his impending duel with Shields—claiming that it was contrary to the Bible and Christianity. He admitted that the dueling code was barbarous and regretted much to find himself in its toils, but said he, "The Bible is not my book, nor Christianity my profession."

In some reminiscences of Lincoln, recently published, referring to a celebrated murder case in which they were counsel for the defendant, Mr. Perkins says: "I reminded him that from the first I had seen, and to him said, the case is hopeless, and that he must have expected to work a miracle to save the accused. He answered that I did him injustice, *since he* had no faith in miracles."

Alluding to Lincoln's alleged change of heart, he writes: "He never changed a sentiment on the subject up to his final sleep."

James Gorley

Mr. Gorley, who was the confidential friend of Lincoln, and who spent much time with him, both at home and abroad, made the following statement: "Lincoln belonged to no religious sect. He was religious in his own way not as others generally. I do not think he ever had a change of heart, religiously speaking.

Had he ever had a change of heart he would have told me. He could not have neglected it."

William Jayne, M.D.

Dr. Jayne, who was appointed Governor of Dakota by Lincoln, is one of the most prominent citizens of Springfield, and was one of Lincoln's ablest and most faithful political friends. He secured Lincoln's nomination for the Legislature once, and was one of the first to pit him against Douglas. In a letter to me, dated August 18, 1887, Dr. Jayne says:

> His general reputation among his neighbors and friends of twenty-five years' standing was that of a disbeliever in the accepted faith of orthodox Christians. His mind was purely logical in its construction and action. He believed nothing except what was susceptible of demonstration. . . . His most intimate friends here, and close to him in the confidential relations of life, assert, in regard to those who claim for Lincoln a faith in the orthodox Christian belief, that the claim is a fraud and utter nonsense.

Hon. Jesse K. Dubois

Jesse K. Dubois, for a time State Auditor of Illinois, a noble and gifted man, and one whom Lincoln dearly loved, once related an anecdote which shows that if Lincoln did believe in a Supreme Being, he had little reverence for the God of Christianity. In company with Dubois, he was visiting a family in or near Springfield. It was summer, and while Dubois was in the house with the family, Lincoln occupied a seat in the yard with his feet resting against a tree, as was his wont. The lady, who was a very zealous Christian, called attention to his appearance and commented rather severely upon his ugliness. When they returned home Dubois referred to the lady's remarks. Lincoln was silent for a moment, and then said: "Dubois, I know that I am ugly, but she worships a God who is uglier than I am."

Hon. Joseph Gillespie

Judge Gillespie, of Edwardsville, Ill., one of Lincoln's most valued friends, writes as follows: "Mr. Lincoln seldom said anything on the subject of religion. He said once to me that he never could reconcile the prescience of Deity with the uncertainty of events."

"It was difficult," says Judge Gillespie, "for him to believe without demonstration."

Judge Stephen T. Logan

Lincoln was admitted to the bar in 1837, when he was twenty-eight years of age, Judge Logan being on the bench at the time. Soon after his admission he formed a partnership with John T. Stuart which existed nearly four years, or until Mr. Stuart entered Congress. He then became the partner of Judge Logan, and continued in business with him until 1843, when he united his practice with that of Mr. Herndon. The testimony of Mr. Stuart and Mr. Herndon has already been given. No formal statement of Judge Logan concerning this question has been preserved. All that I have been able to find is contained in a letter from Mr. Herndon dated Dec. 22, 1888. Mr. Herndon wrote in relation to Lincoln's letter of consolation to his dying father. In Lincoln's letter, while Christ and Christianity are wholly ignored, there is an implied recognition of immortality and an expressed hope that he may meet his father again. Lincoln's friends, for the most part, consider the letter merely conventional, not an expression of his real sentiments, but simply an effort to console his Christian father whom he could never meet again on earth. Mr. Herndon, however, is inclined to believe that while the tone of the letter is not exactly in accordance with the views generally held by Lincoln, it is yet a sincere expression of the feelings he entertained at the time. Referring to this letter, Mr. Herndon says: "I showed the letter to Logan, Stuart, *et al.* Logan laughed in my face as much as to say: 'Herndon, are you so green as to believe that letter to be Lincoln's real ideas?' I cannot give the exact words of Logan, but he in substance said: "Lincoln was an Infidel of the most radical type.'"

Hon. Leonard Swett

I close this division of my evidence with the testimony of that gifted lawyer and honored citizen of Illinois, Leonard Swett. Previous to his removal to Chicago, in 1865, Mr. Swett resided in Bloomington, and for a dozen years traveled the old Eighth Judicial Circuit with Lincoln. Few men knew Lincoln better than did Swett, and none was held in higher esteem by Lincoln than he. It was he who placed Lincoln in nomination for the Presidency at Chicago in 1860. I quote from a letter written by Mr. Swett in 1866:

> You ask me whether he [Lincoln] changed his religious opinions toward the close of his life. I think not. As he became involved in matters of the greatest importance, full of great responsibility and great doubt, a feeling of religious reverence, a belief in God and his justice and overruling providence increased with him. He was always full of natural religion. He believed in God as much as the most approved church member, yet he judged of him by the same system of generalization as he judged everything else. He had very little faith in ceremonials or forms. In fact he cared nothing for the form of anything. . . . If his religion were to be judged by the lines and rules of church creeds, he would fall far short of the standard.

CHAPTER ELEVEN:
Testimony of Friends and Acquaintances of Lincoln Who Knew Him in Illinois
☆ ☆ ☆ ☆

Hon. W.H.T. Wakefield – Hon. D.W. Wilder – Dr. B.F. Gardner
Hon. J.K. Vandemark – A. Jeffrey – Dr. Arch E. McNeal
Charles McGrew – Edward Butler – Joseph Stafford
Judge A.D. Norton – J.L. Morrell – Mahlon Ross – L. Wilson
H.K. Magie – Hon. James Tuttle – Col. F.S. Rutherford
Judge Robert Leachman – Hon. Orin B. Gould – M.S. Gowin
Col. R.G. Ingersoll – Leonard W. Volk – Joseph Jefferson
Hon. E.B. Washburn – Hon. E.M. Haines

I will next present the evidence that I have gleaned from the lips or pens of personal friends of Lincoln who were ac quainted with him in Illinois. The relations of these persons to Lincoln were, for the most part, less intimate than were those of the persons named in the preceding chapter; but all of them enjoyed, in no small degree, his confidence and esteem.

Hon. W.H.T. Wakefield

Mr. Wakefield, our first witness, is a son of the distinguished jurist, Judge J.A. Wakefield. He is a prominent journalist, and was the nominee of the United Labor party, for Vice-President, in the Presidential contest of 1888. In a letter to the author, dated Lawrence, Kan., Sept. 28, 1880, Mr. Wakefield says:

My father, the late Judge J.A. Wakefield, was a life-long

friend of Lincoln's, they having served through the Black Hawk war together and been in the Illinois Legislature together, during which latter time Lincoln boarded with my father in Vandalia, which was then the state capital. I remember of his visiting my father at Galena, in 1844 or 1845. They continued to correspond until Lincoln's death.

My father was a member of the Methodist church and frequently spoke of and lamented Lincoln's Infidelity, and referred to the many arguments between them on the subject.

The noted minister, Peter Cartwright, boarded with my father at the same time that Lincoln did, and my father and mother told me of the many theological and philosophical arguments indulged in by Lincoln and Cartwright, and of the fact that they always attracted many interested listeners and usually ended by Cartwright's getting very angry and the spectators being convulsed with laughter at Lincoln's dry wit and humorous comparisons.

Lincoln's legislative career at Vandalia extended from 1834 to 1837. It was about the beginning of this period that he wrote his book against Christianity. He was thoroughly informed and enthusiastic in his Infidel views, and it is not to be wondered at that on theological questions, he was able to vanquish in debate even so eminent a theologian as Peter Cartwright. Ten years later, Lincoln was the Whig, and Cartwright the Democratic candidate for Congress. In this campaign a determined effort was made by the church to defeat Lincoln on account of his Infidelity. But his popularity, his reputation for honesty, his recognized ability, and his transcendent powers on the stump, carried him successfully through, and he was triumphantly elected.

Hon. D. W. Wilder

One of the most gifted and honorable of Western journalists is D. W. Wilder, of Kansas. He was Surveyor General of Kansas before it was admitted into the Union, and after it became a State, he held the office of State Auditor. Many years ago Gen. Wilder wrote and published an editorial on Lincoln's religious views in which he affirmed that Lincoln was a disbeliever in Christianity. The article excited the wrath of the clergy, among them the Rev. D. P. Mitchell, the leading Methodist divine of Kansas, who replied with much warmth, but without refuting the statements of Gen. Wilder. Some of my Western readers will recall the article and the controversy it provoked. I have been unable to procure a copy of it, but in its place I present the following extract from a letter received from Gen. Wilder, dated St. Joseph, Mo., Dec. 29, 1881: "Lincoln believed in God, but not in the divinity of Christ. At first, like Franklin, he was probably an Atheist. Although a 'forgiving' man himself, he did not believe that any amount of 'penitence' could affect the logical effects of violated law. He has a remarkable passage on that theme."

Concerning Lincoln's partner, Mr. Herndon, with whom he was acquainted, Gen. Wilder says: "Write to Wm. H. Herndon, a noble man, Springfield, Ill. Send him your book [*Life of Paine*]. He will reply. The stories told about him are lies."

B. F. Gardner, M.D.

Dr. Gardner, an old and respected resident of Atlanta, Ill., in March, 1887, made the following statement in regard to Lincoln's views:

> I knew Lincoln from 1854 up to the time he left Springfield. He was an Infidel. He did not change his belief. Herndon told the truth in his lecture. Lincoln did not believe that prayer moved God. When he requested the prayers of his neighbors on leaving Springfield for Washington, he saw that a storm was coming and that he must have the support of the church.

These words of Lincoln in his farewell speech requesting the prayers of his friends, though used merely in a conventional way, have been cited by Holland, Arnold, and others, to prove that he believed in the efficacy of prayer. That no such import was attached to them at the time is admitted by Holland himself. He says:

> This parting address was telegraphed to every part of

the country, and was strangely misinterpreted. So little was the man's character understood that his simple and earnest request that his neighbors should pray for him was received by many as an evidence both of his weakness and his hypocrisy. No President had ever before asked the people, in a public address, to pray for him. It sounded like the cant of the conventicle to ears unaccustomed to the language of piety from the lips of politicians. The request was tossed about as a joke "old Abe's last."[1]

Hon. J. K. Vandemark

J.K. Vandemark, who formerly resided near Springfield, Ill., and who was well acquainted with Lincoln, on the 13th of October, 1887, at Valparaiso, Neb., testified as follows: "I met Lincoln often had many conversations with him in his office. To assert that he was a believer in Christianity is absurd. He had no faith in the dogmas of the church."

Mr. Vandemark at the time his testimony was given was a member of the State Senate of Nebraska.

A. Jeffrey

Mr. Jeffrey, who has resided near Waynesville, Ill., for a period of fifty years, and who was in the habit of attending court with Lincoln, year after year, in an interview on the 1st of March, 1887, made the following statement: "Lincoln was decidedly Liberal. He admitted that he wrote a book against Christianity. In later years he seldom talked on this subject, but he did not change his belief. A thrust at the doctrine of endless punishment always pleased him. This doctrine he abhorred."

Dr. Arch F. McNeall

Dr. McNeall, an old physician of Bowen, Ill., who was a delegate to the Decatur Convention which brought Lincoln forward as a candidate for the Presidency, says: "I met Lincoln often

---

1. Holland's *Life of Lincoln*, p. 254.

during our political campaigns, and was quite well acquainted with him. I know that he was a Liberal thinker."

Charles McGrew

Dr. McGrew is a resident of Coles County, Ill., the county in which nearly all of Lincoln's relatives have resided for sixty years. He is cousin of Hon. Allen G. Thurman, and is a man of sterling character. He was for a time related to Lincoln, in a business way, and met him frequently. I met Dr. McGrew in 1888, and when I propounded the question, "Was Lincoln a Christian?" he replied: "Lincoln was not a Christian. He was cautious and reserved and seldom said anything about religion except when he was alone with a few companions whose opinions were similar to his. On such occasions he did not hesitate to express his unbelief."

Edward Butler

Early in 1858, Lincoln delivered his memorable Springfield speech which prepared the way for his debates with Douglas, and made him President of the United States. Mr. Edward Butler, who resided in Springfield for a period of twenty-six years, and who was well acquainted with Lincoln, was leader of the band which furnished the music on this occasion. In a letter written at Lyons, Kan., Jan. 16, 1890, Mr. Butler relates some incidents connected with the meeting, and quotes a passage from Lincoln's speech to the effect that from the agitation of the slavery question, truth would in the end prevail. Alluding to this passage, Mr. Butler says:

> Shortly after the meeting referred to, I chanced to be talking with Lincoln and quizzingly enquired how he could reconcile this and similar utterances with Holy Writ? Without committing himself, he enquired if I had read Gregg's *Creed of Christendom*. I informed him that I had not. "Then," said he, "read that book and perhaps you may ascertain my views about truth prevailing." I never conversed with Lincoln afterwards, but I ob-

tained the book, which I keep treasured in my library. I am well convinced that no man who is used to weighing evidence, especially of Lincoln's humane and unbiased disposition, can read the book in question without truth coming to the surface.

It is hardly necessary to state that Gregg's *Creed of Christendom* is a standard work in Infidel literature, one of the most scholarly, powerful and convincing arguments against orthodox Christianity ever written.

Joseph Stafford

Joseph Stafford, a resident of Galesburg, Ill., and an acquaintance of Lincoln, says: "I know that Lincoln was a Liberal."

Judge A. D. Norton

In April, 1893, at Ardmore, I.T., I met Judge Norton, of Gainesville, Tex., an old acquaintance of Lincoln and Douglas. Judge Norton related many interesting reminiscences of these noted men. Speaking of Lincoln's religion, he said:

> For nearly fifty years I was a resident of Illinois. I practiced for many years in the same courts with Lincoln and knew him well. He was an Infidel. In his early manhood he wrote a book against Christianity which his friends prevented him from publishing. Because he had become famous, the church preached him from a theatre to heaven.

J. L. Morrell

Mr. J. L. Morrell, a worthy citizen of Virden, Ill., who came to Illinois soon after Lincoln did, settled in the adjoining county to him, and like him followed for a time the avocation of surveyor, in a conversation, with the writer, on the 8th of February, 1889, made the following statement: "I knew Lincoln well – met him often. His religion was the religion of common sense. He went into this subject as deep as any man. He did not believe the inconsistencies of theology. He was not a Christian."

Mahlon Ross, Esq.

Squire Ross, another old resident of Virden, Ill., a lawyer, and a writer of some repute, says: "I was acquainted with Lincoln, but never talked with him on religion. He did not belong to a church, and his friends say that he was not a Christian."

Lusk Wilson

Similar to the above is the testimony of Mr. Lusk Wilson, a prominent and respectable citizen of Litchfield, Ill.: "I was acquainted with Abraham Lincoln, but never heard him give his views on the subject of religion. His partner, Herndon, and other friends, state that he was not a believer in Christianity."

Hon. James Tuttle

Two miles east of Atlanta, Ill., resides one of the pioneers of Illinois, James Tuttle, now over eighty years of age. He was a member of the Constitutional Convention of 1847, and is a man universally esteemed for his love of truth and honesty. Mr. Tuttle's residence is situated on the State road leading from Springfield to Bloomington. In going from Springfield to Bloomington, to attend court, and in returning home again, Lincoln always stopped over night with Mr. Tuttle. Theological questions were favorite topics with both of them, and the evening hours were usually spent in conversations of this character. Mr. Tuttle accordingly became well acquainted with Lincoln's religious views. Feb. 26, 1887, at Minier, Ill., he made the following statement relative to them:

> Mr. Lincoln did not believe in Christianity. He denounced it unsparingly. He had the greatest contempt for religious revivals, and called those who took part in them a set of ignoramuses. He was one of the most ardent admirers of Thomas Paine I ever met. He was continually quoting from the *Age of Reason*. Said he, "I never tire of reading Paine."

Mr. Tuttle is confident that Lincoln always remained a Freethinker, and believes that those who claim to have evidence from him to the contrary, willfully affirm what they know to be false.

H. K. Magie

Mr. Magie formerly lived in Illinois, and was for a time connected with the State Department at Springfield. Writing from Brooklyn, N.Y., March 19, 1888, he says:

> My acquaintance with Mr. Lincoln was limited, as I did not reside in Springfield during his residence there. I met him during his campaign with Douglas at different times, and was with him once for three days. . . . Mr. Lincoln was a Freethinker of the Thomas Paine type. There have been picked up some of Mr. Lincoln's utterances about "Providence," "God," and the like, on which an attempt is made to make him out a Christian. Those who knew him intimately agree in the statement that he was a pronounced skeptic.

Mr. Magie also refers to the Infidel pamphlet written by Lincoln. His knowledge regarding this, however, was derived, not from Lincoln himself, but from his friends. He says: "At one time he wrote a criticism of the New Testament which he proposed to publish and which his friends succeeded in having suppressed, solely because of their regard for his political future."

In a recent contribution to a New York paper from Washington, D.C., Mr. Magie writes as follows:

> I have always been fully persuaded in my own mind that it would have been utterly impossible for a man possessing that intuitive wisdom, keenness of logic, and discernment of truth, which were the marked characteristics of Mr. Lincoln's mind, ever to have subscribed to the atrocious doctrines of the Christian church. He was developed far above it, and although making no war upon the church, he did not hesitate to speak his mind freely upon these subjects upon all proper occasions. I lived in Springfield among his old neighbors for many years, and I have talked with

many of them, and to those who had good opportunity to know his views touching religious matters. All, without exception, classed him among the skeptics. It was not until after his death that he was claimed as a Christian.

I am sorry for Newton Bateman. He has placed himself in a most awkward predicament by trying to keep out of one. . . . He permitted Mr. Holland to circulate an atrocious falsehood in his *Life of Lincoln* rather than incur "unpleasant notoriety" by a firm and courageous denial.

It is not a matter of much importance as to just what Abraham Lincoln did believe concerning God, the Bible, or the man Jesus, but when we discover an earnest, persistent, mean, and wicked attempt by lying and deceitful men to pervert the truth in this matter, in order that their "holy religion" shall profit by their lies, the matter does become of some importance, and I am glad that Mr. — has taken hold of this subject with that zeal and earnestness which usually characterize his great ability, and from what I know in this matter I can assure all whom it may concern that by the time he is through with the subject it will be deemed settled that Mr. Lincoln was not a hypocrite, neither was he a believer in the monstrous and superstitious doctrines of the Christian church.

The foregoing evidence, with the exception of a portion of Mr. Magie's testimony, was all given to the writer by the witnesses themselves, either by letter or orally, and he hereby certifies to its faithful transcription. This evidence is from men whose characters as witnesses cannot be impeached, and it is hardly possible that one of them will ever favor the other side with a disclaimer.

Col. F. S. Rutherford

I wish now to record a statement from Colonel Rutherford, a well-known citizen and soldier of Illinois. It was not made to the writer, but was made during the war to Mr. W. W. Fraser, a member of his regiment, and a man of unquestionable veracity. I will let Mr. Fraser present it, together with the circumstances which called it out. I quote from a letter dated

Ottawa, Kan., Dec. 16, 1881:

> During the siege of Vicksburg our colonel, F.S. Rutherford, Colonel of the 97th Ill. Vol. Inft., was about to leave us, and I went to see him about taking a small package to Alton – his home and mine. He had been sick and quite unable to do active service. During our conversation I said that many of the Alton boys did not like to be left under the command of —. Colonel Rutherford then said: "If my life is worth anything I owe it as much to my family as my country, and it will be worthless to either if I stay much longer in camp, but I hate to leave the boys."
>
> Colonel Rutherford said that he had stumped his district for Mr. Lincoln, and had expected, from Mr. Lincoln's promises, something better than a colonelcy. I told Colonel Rutherford that I was sorry to hear that, as I had always thought so well of Mr. Lincoln. Mr. Rutherford then said: "What more could you expect of an Infidel?"
>
> I said: "Why, Colonel, doesn't Lincoln believe in a God?"
>
> He replied: "Well, he may believe in God, but he doesn't believe in the Bible nor Christ. I know it, for I have heard him make fun of them and say that Christ was a bastard if Joseph was not his father, and I have some sheets of paper now at home that he wrote, making fun of the Bible."

Judge Robert Leachman

The venerable Southern jurist, Judge Leachman, was one of Lincoln's intimate and valued friends. He is a Christian, but candidly confesses that Lincoln was not a believer. In the autumn of 1889, at Anniston, Ala., Judge Leachman made the following statement to Mr. W. S. Andres, of Portsmouth, Ohio:

> Lincoln was not such a Christian as the term is used to imply by church members and church-going people. He was in the strictest sense a moralist. He looked to actions and not to belief. He greatly admired the Golden Rule, and was one of those who thought that "One world at a time" was a good idea. . . . He thought this a good place to be happy as is shown by his wonderful love for liberty and mercy. No, I can truthfully say,

Abraham Lincoln was not a Christian.

Hon. Orin B. Gould

Another friend and admirer of Lincoln was Orin B. Gould, of Franklin Furnace, Ohio. Mr. Gould was one of the noted men of Southern Ohio. He was a man of sterling worth and extensive knowledge, and was familiarly known as the "Sage of the Furnace." He became acquainted with Lincoln in Illinois at an early day, and a close friendship existed between them while Lincoln lived. Mr. Gould survived his illustrious friend nearly a quarter of a century, dying recently at his beautiful home on the banks of the Ohio. Previous to his death the question of Lincoln's religion was presented to him and his own views on the subject solicited. His response was as follows:

> He, like myself, recognized no monsters for Gods. He, like myself, discarded the divinity of Christ, and the idea of a hell's fire. He, like myself, admired Christ as a man, and believed the devil and evil to be simply "truth misunderstood." He, like myself, thought good wherever found should be accepted and the bad rejected.

M.S. Gowin

Mr. Gowin, an old and prominent citizen, and Justice of the Peace, of McCune, Kan., in a recent article, has this to say regarding Lincoln: "I lived near Springfield, Ill., from the time that I was a child, and at the time Lincoln came before the people, and during the time he was President, his enemies called him an Infidel, and his friends did not deny it."

Col. Robert G. Ingersoll

On the eighty-fourth anniversary of Lincoln's birth, Col. Ingersoll delivered in New York his masterly oration on Abraham Lincoln. In this oration he affirmed that the religion of Lincoln was the religion of Voltaire and Paine. Immediately after its delivery Gen. Collis, of New York, addressed the following note to Col. Ingersoll:

Dear Col. Ingersoll:

I have just returned home from listening to your most entertaining lecture upon the life of Abraham Lincoln. I thank you sincerely for all that was good in it, and that entitles me to be frank in condemning what I consider was bad. You say that Lincoln's religion was the religion of Voltaire and Tom Paine. I know not where you get your authority for this, but if the statement be true, Lincoln himself was untrue, for no man invoked "the gracious favor of Almighty God" in every effort of his life with more apparent fervor than did he, and this God was not the Deists' God but the God whom he worshiped under the forms of the Christian Church, of which he was a member.

I do not write this in defense of his religion or as objecting to yours, but I think it were better for the truth of history that you should blame him for what he was than commend him for what he was not.

Sincerely yours,

Charles H. T. Collis

In answer to the above Col. Ingersoll penned the following reply:

Gen. Charles H. T. Collis,

My dear sir:

I have just received your letter in which you criticise a statement made by me to the effect that Lincoln's religion was the religion of Voltaire and Thomas Paine, and you add, "I know not where you get your authority for this, but if the statement be true, Lincoln himself was untrue, for no man ever invoked the gracious favor of Almighty God in every effort of his life with more apparent fervor than did he."

You seem to be laboring under the impression that Voltaire was not a believer in God, and that he could not have invoked the gracious favor of Almighty God. The truth is that Voltaire was not only a believer in God, but even in special Providence. I know that the clergy have always denounced Voltaire as an Atheist, but this can be accounted for in two ways:

(1) By the ignorance of the clergy, and (2) by their contempt of truth. Thomas Paine was also a believer in God, and wrote his creed as follows: "I believe in one God and no more, and hope for immortality."

The ministers have also denounced Paine as an Atheist.

You will, therefore, see that your first statement is without the slightest foundation in fact. Lincoln could be perfectly true to himself if he agreed with the religious sentiments of Voltaire and Paine, and yet invoke the gracious favor of Almighty God.

You also say, "This God" (meaning the God whose favor Lincoln invoked) "was not the Deists' God." The Deists believe in an Infinite Being, who created and preserves the universe. The Christians believe no more. Deists and Christians believe in the same God, but they differ as to what this God has done, and to what this God will do. You further say that "Lincoln worshiped his God under the forms of the Christian Church, of which he was a member." Again you are mistaken. Lincoln was never a member of any church. Mrs. Lincoln stated a few years ago that Mr. Lincoln was not a Christian. Hundreds of his acquaintances have said the same thing. Not only so, but many of them have testified that he was a Freethinker; that he denied the inspiration of the Scriptures, and that he always insisted that Christ was not the son of God, and that the dogma of the atonement was and is an absurdity.

I will very gladly pay you one thousand dollars for your trouble to show that one statement in your letter is correct – even one. And now, to quote you, "Do you not think it were better for the truth of history that you should state the facts about Lincoln, and that you should commend him for what he was rather than for what he was not?"

Yours truly,

R.G. Ingersoll

Leonard W. Volk

In the spring of 1860, just before Lincoln was nominated for the Presidency, the celebrated sculptor, Yolk, made a bust of him. He spent a week in Chicago and made daily sittings in the artist's studio. Mr. Yolk relates the following incident, which hardly accords with the tales told about Lincoln's reverence for the Sabbath, and his love for church services: "He entered my studio on Sunday morning, remarking that a friend at the hotel had invited him to go to church. 'But,' said Mr. Lincoln, 'I thought I'd rather come and sit for the bust. The fact is,' he continued, 'I don't like to hear cut-and-dried sermons.'"

Joseph Jefferson

It is difficult for orthodox Christians to reconcile Lincoln's fondness for the play with his reputed piety. That his last act was a visit to the theater is a fact that stands out in ghastly prominence to them. To break its force they offer various explanations. Some say that he went to avoid the office-seekers; others that Mrs. Lincoln compelled him to go; and still others that he was led there by fate. The truth is he was a frequent attendant at the theater. He went there much oftener than he went to church. The visit of a clergyman annoyed him, but the society of actors he enjoyed. He greatly admired the acting of Edwin Booth. He sent a note to the actor Hackett, praising him for his fine presentation of Falstaff. He called John McCulloch to his box one night and congratulated him on his successful rendition of the part he was playing.

In his autobiography, which recently appeared in the *Century Magazine,* Joseph Jefferson gives some interesting reminiscences of Lincoln. In the earlier part of his dramatic career he was connected with a theatrical company, the managers of which, one of whom was his father, built a theater in Springfield, Ill. A conflict between the preachers and players ensued. The church was powerful then, and the city joined with the church to suppress the theater. The history of the struggle and its termination, as narrated by Mr. Jefferson, is as follows:

> In the midst of their rising fortunes a heavy blow fell upon them. A religious revival was in progress at the time, and the fathers of the church not only launched forth against us in their sermons, but by some political maneuver got the city to pass a new law enjoining a heavy license against our "unholy" calling; I forget the amount, but it was large enough to be pro-

hibitory. Here was a terrible condition of affairs – all our available funds invested, the Legislature in session, the town full of people, and by a heavy license denied the privilege of opening the new theater!

In the midst of their trouble a young lawyer called on the managers. He had heard of the injustice, and offered, if they would place the matter in his hands, to have the license taken off, declaring that he only desired to see fair play, and he would accept no fee whether he failed or succeeded. The case was brought up before the council. The young man began his harangue. He handled the subject with tact, skill, and humor, tracing the history of the drama from the time when Thespis acted in a cart to the stage of to-day. He illustrated his speech with a number of anecdotes, and kept the council in a roar of laughter; his good humor prevailed, and the exorbitant tax was taken off.

This young lawyer was very popular in Springfield, and was honored and beloved by all who knew him, and, after the time of which I write, he held rather an important position in the Government of the United States. He now lies buried near Springfield, under a monument commemorating his greatness and his virtues and his name was Abraham Lincoln.

Hon. Elihu B. Washburn

The ball-room, too, had its attractions for him. Some years ago Hon. E.B. Washburn contributed to the *North American Review* a lengthy article on Lincoln. When President Taylor was inaugurated, Lincoln was serving his term in Congress. Alluding to the inaugural ball, Mr. Washburn says: "A small number of mutual friends including Mr. Lincoln made up a party to attend the inauguration ball together. It was by far the most brilliant inauguration ball ever given. . . . We did not take our departure until three or four o'clock in the morning."[2]

Hon. Elijah M. Harris

In February, 1859, Governor Bissell gave a reception in

---

2. *Reminiscences of Lincoln*, p. 19.

Springfield which Lincoln attended. Hon. E. M. Haines, then a member of the Legislature, and one of Lincoln's supporters for the Senate, referring to the affair, says: "Dancing was going on in the adjacent rooms, and Mr. Lincoln invited my wife to join him in the dancing, which she did, and he apparently took much pleasure in the recreation."[3]

Early in January, 1863, President and Mrs. Lincoln gave a reception and ball at the White House. This was a severe shock to the Christians of the country, and provoked a storm of censure from the religious press.

According to Ninian Edwards, Lincoln is converted to Christianity about 1848. In March, 1849, he attends the inauguration ball and "Won't go home till morning." According to Dr. Smith, he is converted in 1858. In February, 1859, he attends and participates in a ball at Springfield. According to Noah Brooks, he is converted in 1862. In January, 1863, be gives a ball himself. In every instance he retires from the altar only to enter the ball-room.

---

3. *Every-Day Life of Lincoln*, p. 308.

CHAPTER TWELVE
Testimony of Friends and Acquaintances of Lincoln Who Knew Him in Washington
☆ ☆ ☆ ☆

Hon. Geo. W. Julian – Hon. John B. Alley – Hon. Hugh McCulloch
Donn Piatt – Hon. Schuyler Colfax – Hon. Geo. S. Boutwell
Hon. Wm. D. Kelly – E.H. Wood – Dr. J.J. Thompson
Rev. James Shrigley – Hon. John Covode – Jas. E. Murdock
Hon. M.B. Field – Harriet Beecher Stowe – Hon. J.P. Usher
Hon. S.P. Chase – Frederick Douglas – Mr. Defrees
Hon. Wm. H. Seward – Judge Aaron Goodrich – Nicolay and Hay's
Life of Lincoln – Warren Chase – Hon. A.J. Grover
Judge James M. Nelson

The evidence of more than fifty witnesses has already been adduced to prove that Lincoln was not a Christian in Illinois. Those who at first were so forward to claim that he was, have generally recognized the futility of the claim. They have abandoned it, and content themselves with affirming that he became a Christian after he went to Washington. These claimants, being for the most part rigid sectarians themselves, endeavor to convince the world that he not only became a Christian, but an orthodox Christian, and a sectarian; that even from a Calvinistic standpoint, he was "sound not only on the truth of the Christian religion, but on all its fundamental doctrines and teachings." The testimony of Colonel Lamon, Judge Davis, Mrs. Lincoln, and Colonel Nicolay, not only refutes this claim, but shows that he was not in any just sense of the term a Christian when he died. In addition to this evidence, I will now present the testimony of a score of other witnesses who knew him in Washington. These witnesses do not all affirm that he was a total disbeliever in Christianity; but a part of them do, while the testimony of the remainder is to the effect that he was not orthodox as claimed.

Hon. George W. Julian

Our first witness is George W. Julian, of Indiana. Mr. Julian was for many years a leader in Congress, was the Anti-Slavery candidate for Vice-President, in 1852, and one of the founders of the party that elected Lincoln to the Presidency. He was one of Lincoln's warmest personal friends and intimately acquainted with him at Washington. Writing to me from Santa Fe, N.M., under date of March 13, 1888, Mr. Julian says:

> I knew him [Lincoln] well, and I know that he was not a Christian in any old-fashioned orthodox sense of the word, but only a religious Theist. He was, substantially, such a Christian as Jefferson, Franklin, Washington, and John Adams; and it is perfectly idle to assert the contrary.

Hon. John B. Alley

In 1886, the publishers of the *North American Review* issued one of the most unique, original, and interesting works on Lincoln that has yet appeared – *Reminiscences of Abraham Lincoln*. It was edited by Allen Thorndike Rice, and comprises, in addition to a biographical sketch of Lincoln's life, by the editor, thirty-three articles on Lincoln written by as many distinguished men of his day. One of the best articles in this volume is from the pen of one of Boston's merchant princes, John B. Alley. Mr. Alley was for eight years a member of Congress from Massachusetts, serving in this capacity during all the years that Lincoln was President. To his ability and integrity as a statesman this remarkable yet truthful tribute has been paid: "No bill he ever reported and no measure he ever advocated during his long term of service failed to receive the approbation of the House." Lincoln recognized his many sterling qualities, and throughout the war his relations with the President were of the most intimate character. Mr. Alley is one of the many who know that Lincoln was not a Christian, and one of the few who have the courage to affirm it. He says:

> In his religious views Mr. Lincoln was very nearly what we would call a Freethinker. While he reflected a great deal upon religious subjects he communicated his thoughts to a very few. He had little faith in the popular religion of the times. He had a broad conception of the goodness and power of an over-ruling Providence, and said to me one day that he felt sure the Author of our being, whether called God or Nature, it mattered little which, would deal very mercifully with poor erring humanity in the other, and he hoped better, world. He was as free as possible from all sectarian thought, feeling, or sentiment. No man was more tolerant of the opinions and feelings of others in the direction of religious sentiment or had less faith in religious dogmas.[1]

In conclusion, Mr. Alley says: "While Mr. Lincoln was perfectly honest and upright and led a blameless life, he was in no sense what might be considered a religious man."[2]

Hon. Hugh McCulloch

Hon. Hugh McCulloch, a member of Lincoln's Cabinet, his last Secretary of the Treasury, writes:

> Grave and sedate in manner, he was full of kind and gentle emotion. He was fond of poetry. Shakespeare was his delight. Few men could read with equal expression the plays of the great dramatist. The theater had great attractions for him, but it was comedy, not tragedy, he went to hear. He had great enjoyment of the plays that made him laugh, no matter how absurd and grotesque, and he gave expression to his enjoyment by hearty and noisy applause. He was a man of strong religious

---

1. *Reminiscences of Lincoln*, pp. 590, 591.
2. *Ibid.*

convictions, but he cared nothing for the dogmas of the churches and had little respect for their creeds.[3]

Donn Piatt

The distinguished lawyer, soldier and journalist, Donn Piatt, who knew Lincoln in Illinois and who met him often in Washington, writes: "I soon discovered that this strange and strangely gifted man, while not at all cynical, was a skeptic. His view of human nature was low, but good-natured. I could not call it suspicious, but he believed only what he saw."[4]

Those who are disposed to believe that Lincoln's Christian biographers have observed an inflexible adherence to truth in their statements concerning his religious belief would do well to ponder the following words of Mr. Piatt:

> History is after all, the crystallization of popular beliefs. As a pleasant fiction is more acceptable than a naked fact, and as the historian shapes his wares, like any other dealer, to suit his customers, one can readily see that our chronicles are only a duller sort of fiction than the popular novels so eagerly read; not that they are true, but that they deal in what we long to have the truth. Popular beliefs, in time, come to be superstitions, and create gods and devils. Thus Washington is deified into an impossible man, and Aaron Burr has passed into a like impossible monster. Through the same process Abraham Lincoln, one of our truly great, has almost gone from human knowledge.[5]

Hon. Schuyler Colfax

Previous to the war no class of persons were louder in their denunciation of Abolitionism than the clergy of the North. When at last it became evident that the institution of slavery was

---

3. *Ibid.*, pp. 412, 413.

4. *Ibid.*, p. 480.

5. *Ibid*, p. 478.

doomed, in their eagerness to be found on the popular side, they were equally loud in their demands for its immediate extirpation. In September, 1862, a deputation of Chicago clergymen waited upon the President for the purpose of urging him to proclaim the freedom of the slave. Notwithstanding he had matured his plans and was ready to issue his Proclamation, he gave them no intimation of his intention. In connection with their visit, Colfax relates the following:

> One of these ministers felt it his duty to make a more searching appeal to the President's conscience. Just as they were retiring, he turned, and said to Mr. Lincoln, "What you have said to us, Mr. President, compels me to say to you in reply, that it is a message to you from our Divine Master, through me, commanding you, sir, to open the doors of bondage that the slave may go free!"
>
> Mr. Lincoln replied, instantly, "That may be, sir, for I have studied this question, by night and by day, for weeks and for months, but if it is, as you say, a message from your Divine Master, is it not odd that the only channel he could send it by was that roundabout route by that awfully wicked city of Chicago?"[6]

In a lecture delivered in Brooklyn, N.Y., in 1886, Mr. Colfax stated that Lincoln was not a Christian, in the evangelical sense. To a gentleman who visited him at his home in South Bend, Ind., he declared that Lincoln was not a believer in orthodox Christianity. Again at Atchison, Kan., he informed Mr. Perkins that Lincoln had never been converted to Christianity, as claimed.

Hon. William D. Kelley

William D. Kelley, for thirty years a member of Congress from Pennsylvania, relates an incident similar to the one related by Mr. Colfax. A "Quaker preacher" called at the White House to urge the President to proclaim at once the freedom of the slave. To illustrate her argument and emphasize her plea, she cited the

---

6. *Ibid.*, pp. 334, 335.

history of Deborah. Mr. Kelley says:

> Having elaborated this Biblical example, the speaker assumed that the President was, as Deborah had been, the appointed minister of the Lord, and proceeded to tell him that it was his duty to follow the example of Deborah, and forthwith abolish slavery, and establish freedom throughout the land, as the Lord had appointed him to do:
>
> "Has the Friend finished?" said the President, as she ceased to speak. Having received an affirmative answer, he said: "I have neither time nor disposition to enter into discussion with the Friend, and end this occasion by suggesting for her consideration the question whether, if it be true that the Lord has appointed me to do the work she has indicated, it is not probable that he would have communicated knowledge of the fact to me as well as to her."[7]

Hon. George S. Boutwell

A great many pious stories have been circulated in regard to the Emancipation Proclamation. We are told that he made a "solemn vow to God" that if Lee was defeated at Antietam he would issue the Preliminary Proclamation. And yet this document contains no recognition of God. He even completed the draft of it on what Christians are pleased to regard as God's holy day. Mr. Boutwell states that Lincoln once related to him the circumstances attending the promulgation of the instrument. He quotes the following as Lincoln's words:

> The truth is just this: When Lee came over the river, I made a resolution that if McClellan drove him back I would send the Proclamation after him. The battle of Antietam was fought Wednesday, and until Saturday I could not find out whether we had gained a victory or lost a battle. It was then too late to issue the Proclamation that day, and the fact is *I fixed it up a little Sunday,* and Monday I let them have it.[8]

---

7. *Ibid.*, pp. 284, 285.

8. *Ibid.*, p. 126.

E. H. Wood

Mr. E. H. Wood, one of Lincoln's old Springfield neighbors, who visited him at Washington during the war, made the following statement to Mr. Herndon, in October, 1881:

> I came from Auburn, N. Y. – knew Seward well – knew Lincoln very well – lived for three years just across the alley from his residence. I had many conversations with him on politics and religion as late as 1859 and '60. He was a broad religionist – a Liberal. Lincoln told me Franklin's story. Franklin and a particular friend made an agreement that when the first one died he would come back and tell how things went. Well, Franklin's friend died, but never came back. "It is a doubtful question," said Lincoln, "whether we get anywhere to get back." Lincoln said, "There is no hell." He did not say much about heaven. I met him in Washington and saw no change in him.

I have given the testimony of two of Lincoln's nearest neighbors in Springfield – Isaac Hawley and E. H. Wood. Mr. Hawley *believes* that Lincoln was a Christian; Mr. Wood *knows* that he was not. Mr. Hawley never heard Lincoln utter a word to support his belief; Mr. Wood obtained his knowledge from Lincoln himself. Mr. Hawley's belief is of little value compared with Mr. Wood's knowledge. Mr. Hawley never heard Lincoln defend Christianity and probably never heard him oppose it. Lincoln knew that Mr. Hawley was a Christian – that he had no sympathy with his Freethought views. He did not desire to offend or antagonize him, and hence he refrained from introducing a subject that he knew was distasteful to him. Mr. Wood, on the other hand, was a man of broad and Liberal ideas, and Lincoln did not hesitate to express to him his views with freedom.

J. J. Thompson, M.D.

Dr. J. J. Thompson, an old resident of Illinois, now in Colorado, in a letter, dated March 18, 1888, writes as follows: "I knew Abraham Lincoln from my boyhood up to the time of his death. I was in his law office many times and met him several times in Washington. He was a Liberal, outspoken, and seemed to feel proud of it."

"This great and good man," concludes Dr. Thompson, "claimed Humanity as his religion."

Rev. James Shrigley

Rev. Jas. Shrigley, of Philadelphia, who was acquainted with President Lincoln in Washington, and who received a hospital chaplaincy from him, says: "President Lincoln was also remarkably tolerant. He was the friend of all, and never, to my knowledge, gave the influence of his great name to encourage sectarianism in any of its names and forms."[9]

Hon. John Covode

In connection with Mr. Shrigley's appointment, the following anecdote is related. Mr. Shrigley was not orthodox, and when it became known that his name had been sent to thc Senate, a Committee of "Young Christians" waited upon the President for the purpose of inducing him to withdraw the nomination. Hon. John Covode, of Pennsylvania, was present during the interview and gave it to the press. It is as follows:

> "We have called, Mr. President, to confer with you in regard to the appointment of Mr. Shrigley, of Philadelphia, as hospital chaplain."
>
> The President responded: "Oh, yes, gentlemen – I have sent his name to the Senate, and he will no doubt be confirmed at an early day."
>
> One of the young men replied: "We have not come to ask for the appointment, but to solicit you to withdraw the nomination."
>
> "Ah, said Lincoln, "that alters the case; but on what ground do you ask the nomination withdrawn?"

---

9. *Lincoln Memorial Album*, p. 335.

The answer was, "Mr. Shrigley is not sound in his theological opinions."

The President inquired: "On what question is the gentleman unsound?"

Response: "He does not believe in endless punishment; not only so, sir, but he believes that even the rebels themselves will finally be saved."

"Is that so?" inquired the President.

The members of the committee both responded, "Yes," "Yes."

"Well, gentlemen, if that be so, and there is any way under heaven whereby the rebels can be saved, then, for God's sake and their sakes, let the man be appointed."[10]

And he was appointed.

John W. Murdoch

It is claimed that few public men have made greater use of the Bible than Lincoln. This is true. He was continually quoting Scripture or alluding to Scriptural scenes and stories, sometimes to illustrate or adorn a serious speech, but more frequently to point or emphasize a joke. The venerable actor and elocutionist, James E. Murdoch, who had met Lincoln, both in Springfield and Washington, relates an anecdote of him while at Washington which serves to illustrate this propensity:

One day a detachment of troops was marching along the avenue singing the soul-stirring strain of "John Brown." They were walled in on either side by throngs of citizens and strangers, whose voices mingled in the roll of the mighty war-song. In the midst of this exciting scene, a man had clambered into a small tree, on the sidewalk, where he clung, unmindful of the jeers of the passing crowd, called forth by the strange antics he was unconsciously exhibiting in his efforts to overcome the swaying motion of the slight stem which bent beneath his weight. Mr. Lincoln's attention was attracted for a moment, and

10. *Lincoln Memorial Album*, pp. 336, 337.

he paused in the serious conversation in which he was deeply interested and in an abstracted manner, yet with a droll cast of the eye, and a nod of the head in the direction of the man, he repeated, in his dry and peculiar utterance, the following old-fashioned couplet: "And Zaccheous he did climb a tree, His Lord and Master for to see."[11]

Mr. Murdoch states that in connection with this incident, Lincoln was charged "with turning sacred subjects into ridicule." He apologizes for, and attempts to palliate this levity, and affects to believe that Lincoln was a Christian. But almost daily Lincoln indulged in jokes at the expense of the Bible and Christianity, many of them ten-fold more sacrilegious in their character than this trifling incident related by Mr. Murdoch. If the scrupulously pious considered this simple jest, uttered in the midst of a mixed crowd, irreverent, what would have been their horror could they have listened to some of his remarks made when alone with a skeptical boon companion? With Christians and with strangers he was generally guarded in his speech, lest he should give offense; but with his unbelieving friends, up to the end of his career, his keenest shafts of wit were not infrequently aimed at the religion of his day. This shows that the popular faith had no more sacredness for Lincoln, the President, in Washington, than it had for Lincoln, the farmer's boy, who mocked and mimicked it in Indiana, or Lincoln, the lawyer, who scoffed at it and argued against it in Illinois.

Hon. Maunsell B. Field

Mr. Field, who had met nearly all the noted characters of his day, both of Europe and America, in his *Memories of Many Men*, has this significant sentence respecting Lincoln: "Mr. Lincoln was entirely deficient in what the *phrenologists call reverence [veneration].*"
This made it easy for him to emancipate himself from the slavery of priestcraft and become and remain a Freethinker. Pro-

---

11. *Lincoln Memorial Album*, pp. 349, 350.

fessor Beall, one of the ablest of living phrenological writers, says:

"No man can enjoy religion," as the Methodists express it, unless he has well developed veneration and wonder. . . . All those who rebel against any form of government which in childhood they were taught to revere, must of necessity do so in opposition to the faculty of veneration. Thus it is obvious that the less one possesses of the conservative restraining faculties, the more easily he becomes a rebel or an Infidel to that which his reason condemns. On the other hand, the profoundly conscientious and reverential man, who sincerely regards unbelief as a sin, of course instinctively antagonizes every skeptical thought, and is thus likely to remain a slave to the religion learned at his mother's knee.[12]

Mr. Field also relates the following anecdote of Lincoln:

I was once in Mr. Lincoln's company when a sectarian controversy arose. He himself looked very grave, and made no observation until all the others had finished what they had to say. Then with a twinkle of the eye he remarked that he preferred the Episcopalians to every other sect, because they are equally indifferent to a man's religion and his politics.

Harriet Beecher Stowe

The noted author of *Uncle Tom's Cabin* had several interviews with the President. She wrote an article on him which has been cited in proof of his "deeply religious nature." But if her words prove anything, they prove that he was not an evangelical Christian. They are as follows:

But Almighty God has granted to him that clearness of vision which he gives to the true-hearted, and enabled him to set his honest foot in that promised land of freedom which is to be the patrimony of all men, black and white; and from henceforth nations shall rise up and call him blessed. *We believe he*

---

12. *The Brain and the Bible*, pp. 109, 228.

has never made any religious profession, but we see evidence that in passing through this dreadful national crisis, he has been forced by the very anguish of the struggle to look upward, where any rational creature must look for support. No man in this agony has suffered more and deeper, albeit with a dry, weary, patient pain, that seemed to some like insensibility. "Whichever way it ends," he said to the writer, "I have the impression that *I* shan't last long after it's over."[13]

Mrs. Stowe was herself an orthodox Christian communicant, but her store of good sense was too great to allow her to inflict her religious notions upon the unbelieving President, and, as a consequence, she did not see him rush out of the room with a Bible under his arm to – I was going to say – pray to God to deliver him from an intolerable nuisance.

That the mighty burden which pressed upon Lincoln made him a sadder and more serious man at Washington than he had been before is true. Christians are always mistaking sadness for penitence and seriousness for piety, and so they claim that he experienced a change of heart.

Hon. John P. Usher

Christians and Theists are wont to speak of Lincoln's constant and firm reliance upon God. But it is a little remarkable that in the preparation of his greatest work he did not rely upon God. In the supreme moments of his life he forgot God. Dr. Barrows says: "When he wrote his immortal Proclamation, he invoked upon it . . . 'the gracious favor of Almighty God.'" When he wrote his immortal Proclamation he had no thought of God. Judge Usher, a member of his Cabinet, tells us how God came to be invoked:

> In the preparation of the final Proclamation of Emancipation, of January 1, 1863, Mr. Lincoln manifested great solicitude. He had his original draft printed and furnished each member of

---

13. *Every-Day Life of Lincoln,* pp. 575, 576.

his Cabinet with a copy, with the request that each should examine, criticise, and suggest any amendments that occurred to
them. At the next meeting of the Cabinet, Mr. Chase said: "This
paper is of the utmost importance greater than any state paper
ever made by this Government. A paper of so much importance,
and involving the liberties of so many people, ought, I think, to
make some reference to Deity. I do not observe anything of the
kind in it." Mr. Lincoln said: "No; I overlooked it. Some reference to Deity must be inserted. Mr. Chase, won't you make a
draft of what you think ought to be inserted?" Mr. Chase promised to do so, and at the next meeting presented the following:
"And upon this Act, sincerely believed to be an act of justice
warranted by the Constitution upon military necessity, I invoke
the considerate judgment of mankind and the gracious favor of
Almighty God."[14]

Hon. Salmon P. Chase

In the *New York Tribune* of Feb. 22d, 1893, appeared an
article on "How the Emancipation Proclamation was made,"
written by Mrs. Janet Chase Hoyt, daughter of Salmon P. Chase.
In this article Mrs. Hoyt gives the following extract from a letter
written to her by her father in 1867:

Looking over old papers, I found many of my memo-
randa, *etc.*, of the war, and among them my draft of a proclamation of emancipation submitted to Mr. Lincoln the day before
his own was issued. He asked all of us for suggestions in regard
to its form and I submitted mine in writing, and, among other
sentences, the close as it now stands, which he adopted from
my draft with a modification. It may be interesting to you to see
precisely what I said, and I copy it. You must remember that in
the original draft there was no reference whatever to Divine or
human sanction of the act. What I said was this at the conclusion of my letter: "Finally, I respectfully suggest that on an
occasion of such interest there can be no imputation of affecta-
tion against a solemn recognition of responsibility before men
and before God, and that some such close as this will be proper:

---

14. *Reminiscences of Lincoln*, pp. 91, 92.

'And upon this act, sincerely believed to be an act of justice warranted by the Constitution (and of duty demanded by the circumstances of the country), I invoke the considerate judgment of mankind and the gracious favor of Almighty God.' Mr. Lincoln adopted this close, substituting only for the words inclosed in parentheses these words: 'upon military necessity,' which I think was not an improvement.'"

Mr. Defrees

During his Presidency the clergy petitioned him to recommend in his message to Congress an amendment to the Constitution recognizing the existence of God. In preparing his message it seems that he inserted the request. Referring to this, Mr. Defrees, Superintendent of Public Printing during Lincoln's administration, says: "When I assisted him in reading the proof he struck it out, remarking that he had not made up his mind as to its propriety."[15]

Hon. William H. Seward

In his *Travels Around the World*, Seward records one of Lincoln's sarcastic hits at the doctrine of endless punishment. Speaking of England's jealousy of the United States in certain matters, Seward says:

That hesitation and refusal recall President Lincoln's story of the intrusion of the Universalists into the town of Springfield. The several orthodox churches agreed that their pastors should preach down the heresy. One of them began his discourse with these emphatic words: "My Brethren, there is a dangerous doctrine creeping in among us. There are those who are teaching that all men will be saved; but my dear brethren, *we* hope for better things."[16]

---

15. *Westminster Review*, Sept. 1891.
16. *Travels Around the World*, p. 513.

Judge Aaron Goodrich

Judge Goodrich, of Minnesota, Lincoln's minister to Belgium, who was one of the most accomplished scholars in the West, and an author of note, and who was on terms of close intimacy with Lincoln, both before and after he became President, says: "He [Lincoln] believed in a God, *i.e.,* Nature; but he did not believe in the Christ, nor did he ever affiliate with any church."

Frederick Douglass

Abraham Lincoln believed in a Supreme Being, but he did not believe in the God of Christians. The God of Christians was to him the most hideous monster that the imagination of man had ever conceived. There were two doctrines taught in connection with this deity which he especially abhorred – the doctrine of endless punishment, and the doctrine of vicarious atonement. That the innocent should suffer for the guilty – that God should permit his sinless son to be put to a cruel death to atone for the sins of wicked men – was to him an act of the most infamous injustice. His whole nature rebelled against the idea. Frederick Douglass narrates an incident which, while it has no direct reference to this theological doctrine, yet tends to disclose his abhorrence of the idea. Mr. Douglass was engaged in recruiting colored troops and visited the President for the purpose of securing from him a pledge that colored soldiers would be allowed the same privileges accorded white soldiers. As the Confederate Government had declared that they would be treated as insurgents, he also urged upon him the necessity of retaliating, if colored prisoners were put to death. But to the latter proposition Lincoln would not listen. Mr. Douglass says:

> I shall never forget the benignant expression of his face, the tearful look of his eye and the quiver of his voice, when he deprecated a resort to retaliatory measures. He said he could not take men out and kill them in cold blood for what was done by others. If he could get hold of the persons who were guilty of killing the colored prisoners in cold blood, the case would be

different, but *he could not kill the innocent for the guilty.*[17]

Nicolay and Hay's *Life of Lincoln*

Of the numerous biographies of Lincoln that have been published, the authors of three, above all others, were specially qualified and possessed the necessary materials for a reliable biography of him – Herndon, Lamon, and Nicolay and Hay.

As Colonel Lamon's *Life* covers but a part of Lincoln's career, and as Mr. Herndon's *Life* deals more with his private life than with his public history, the biography of Lincoln that is likely to be accepted as the standard authority, is the work written by his private secretaries, Col. John G. Nicolay and Col. John Hay, which originally appeared in the *Century Magazine.* In the chapter on "Lincoln and the Churches," the religious phase of Lincoln's character is presented. In dealing with this question the authors have carefully avoided the rock upon which Lamon's *Life* was wrecked, and at the same time have refrained from repeating the misrepresentations of Holland and Arnold. They do not offend the church by openly declaring that Lincoln was an Infidel; neither do they outrage truth by asserting that he was a Christian. They affirm that during the latter years of his life he recognized a "superior power," but they do not intimate that he recognized Jesus Christ as this power, or any part of it, nor that he accepted the Bible as a special revelation of this power. In the following passage they impliedly deny both his alleged Atheism and his alleged orthodoxy:

> We have no purpose of attempting to formulate his creed; we question if he himself ever did so. There have been swift witnesses who, judging from expressions uttered in his callow youth, have called him an Atheist, and others who, with the most laudable intentions, have remembered improbable conversations which they bring forward to prove at once his orthodoxy and their own intimacy with him.

---

17. *Reminiscences of Lincoln*, pp. 188, 189.

As it is not claimed that Lincoln was an Atheist, especially during the last years of his life, the above can very properly be brought forward in support of the negative of this question. In the last clause it is intended by the authors to administer a sarcastic rebuke to such witnesses as Brooks, Willets and Vinton, as well as deny the truthfulness of their statements.

In regard to Lincoln's youth, the following from Nicolay and Hay's work corroborates Lamon's statements and refutes those of Holland:

> We are making no claim of early saintship for him. He was merely a good boy, with sufficient wickedness to prove his humanity. . . . It is also reported that he sometimes impeded the celerity of harvest operations by making burlesque speeches, or worse than that, comic sermons, from the top of some tempting stump, to the delight of the hired hands and the exasperation of the farmer.

Hon. Warren Chase

In 1888, I received a brief letter from Warren Chase pertaining to Lincoln's religious belief. Mr. Chase was acquainted with Lincoln in Washington. His letter has been mislaid, but I recall the principal points in it, which are as follows: 1. Lincoln was not a believer in Christianity; 2. He was much interested in the phenomena of Spiritualism.

Hon. A.J. Grover

A.J. Grover, a life-long reformer, an old-time Abolitionist, an able advocate of human liberty, and a personal friend and admirer of Lincoln, in a letter written April 13, 1888, sends me the following as his testimony:

> Mr. Lincoln was not a religious man in the church sense. He was an Agnostic. He did not believe in the Bible as the infallible word of God. He believed that Nature is God's word, given to all men in a universal language which is equally

accessible to all, if all are equally intelligent. That this great lesson, God's word in his works, is infinite, and that men have only learned a very little of it, and have yet the most to learn. That the religions of all ages and peoples are only very feeble and imperfect attempts to solve the great problems involved in nature and her laws. Mr. Lincoln heartily disliked the narrow and silly pretensions of the church and priesthood who now falsely claim him, as they do Washington, Franklin and others.

I knew Mr. Lincoln from the Douglas campaign in Illinois in 1858 until his death, and I never heard him on any occasion use a single pious expression in the sense of the church – not a word that indicated that he believed in the church theology. But I have heard him use many expressions that indicated that he did not know much, or pretend to know much, and had no settled convictions concerning the great questions that theology deals so flippantly with, and pretends to know all about. And I know to my own knowledge that the claim the church now sets up that he was a Christian is false – as false as it is in regard to Washington.

Writing to me again under date of Jan. 12, 1889, Mr. Grover says:

> I knew Mr. Lincoln in Illinois and in Washington. I was in the War office, for a time, in a department which had charge of the President's books, so-called. I met him in passing between the White House and the buildings then occupied by the War Department, almost everyday. I often had to go to Mr. Stanton's, office, and have often seen Mr. Lincoln there. I frequently had to go to the White House to see him. It was known to all of his acquaintances that he was a Liberal or Rationalist.

Judge James M. Nelson

The last, and in some respects the most important, of our Washington witnesses is Judge James M. Nelson. Judge Nelson for many years has been a resident of New York, but he formerly lived in Kentucky and Illinois, Lincoln's native and adopted States. He is a son of Thomas Pope Nelson, a distinguished member of Congress from Kentucky, and the first United States

Minister to Turkey. His great grandfather was Thomas Nelson, Jr., a signer of the Declaration of Independence from Virginia. He was long and intimately acquainted with Lincoln both in Illinois and Washington. About the close of 1886, or early in 1887, Judge Nelson published his *Reminiscences of Abraham Lincoln* in the Louisville, Ky., *Times*. In reference to Lincoln's religious opinions he says:

> In religion, Mr. Lincoln was about of the same belief as Bob Ingersoll, and there is no account of his ever having changed. He went to church a few times with his family while he was President, but so far as I have been able to find out he remained an unbeliever.
>
> Mr. Lincoln in his younger days wrote a book in which he endeavored to prove the fallacy of the plan of salvation and the divinity of Christ.

I have yet another passage from Judge Nelson's *Reminiscences* to present, a passage which, more than anything else in this volume, perhaps, is calculated to provoke the wrath of Christian claimants. To lend an air of plausibility to their claims these claimants are continually citing expressions of a seemingly semi-pious character occasionally to be met with in his speeches and state papers. These expressions, in a measure accounted for by Mr. Herndon, Colonel Lamon, and others, are still further explained by a revelation from his own lips. Judge Nelson says: "I asked him once about his fervent Thanksgiving Message and twitted him with being an unbeliever in what was published. 'Oh,' said he, 'that is some of Seward's nonsense, and it pleases the fools.'"

CHAPTER THIRTEEN:
Other Testimony and Opinions
☆ ☆ ☆ ☆

New York World – Boston Globe – Chicago Herald – Manford's
Magazine – Herald and Review – Chambers's Encyclopedia
Encyclopedia Britannica – People's Library of Information
The World's Sages – Every-Day Life of Lincoln – Hon. Jesse W.
Weik – Chas. W. French – Cyrus O. Poole – A Citizen of
Springfield – Henry Walker – Wm. Bissett – Frederick Heath
Rev. Edward Eggleston – Rev. Robert Collyer – Allen Thorndike
Rice – Robert C. Adams – Theodore Stanton – Geo. M. McCrie
Gen. M. M. Trumbull – Rev. David Swing, D.D. – Rev. J. Lloyd
Jones – Rev. John W. Chadwick

The matter selected for this chapter is of a miscellaneous nature, consisting of the statements of those who, for the most part, are not known to have been personally acquainted with Lincoln. It embraces the opinions of journalists, encyclopedists, biographers, and others. If their words cannot be accepted as the testimony of competent witnesses, they may at least be regarded as the verdict of honest jurors.

New York World

In the *New York World,* fifteen years ago, appeared the following:

> While it may fairly be said that Mr. Lincoln entertained many Christian sentiments, it cannot be said that he was himself a Christian in faith or practice. He was no disciple of Jesus of

Nazareth. He did not believe in his divinity and was not a member of his church.

He was at first a writing Infidel of the school of Paine and Volney, and afterward a talking Infidel of the school of Parker and Channing.

Alluding to the friendly attitude he assumed toward the church and Christianity during the war, this article concludes:

If the churches had grown cold – if the Christians had taken a stand aloof – that instant the Union would have perished. Mr. Lincoln regulated his religious manifestations accordingly. He declared frequently that he would do *anything* to save the Union, and among the many things he did was the partial concealment of his individual religious opinions. Is this a blot upon his fame? Or shall we all agree that it was a conscientious and patriotic sacrifice?

Boston Globe

As evidence of Lincoln's piety, we are referred to a picture where Lincoln, with his son Tad, is supposed to be reverentially poring over the pages of the Bible. The history of this picture, however, has often been explained, and its apparently religious character shown to be quite secular. The *Boston Globe,* in a recent issue, says:

The pretty little story about the picture of President Lincoln and his son Tad reading the Bible is now corrected for the one-hundredth time. The Bible was Photographer Brady's picture album, which the President was examining with his son while some ladies stood by. The artist begged the President to remain quiet and the picture was taken. The truth is better than fiction, even if its recital conflicts with a pleasing theory.

Chicago Herald

During February, 1892, the *Chicago Herald* published an editorial on Lincoln's religion. Being one of the latest contribu-

tions to this subject, and appearing in one of the principal journals of Lincoln's own State, it is of especial importance. It is a
candid statement of what nearly every journalist of Illinois
knows or believes to be the facts. From it I quote as follows:

> He was without faith in the Bible or its teachings. On
> this point the testimony is so overwhelming that there is no
> basis for doubt. In his early life Lincoln exhibited a powerful
> tendency to aggressive Infidelity. But when he grew to be a
> politician he became secretive and non-committal in his reli-
> gious belief. He was shrewd enough to realize the necessity of
> reticence with the convictions he possessed if he hoped to suc-
> ceed in politics.
>
> It is matter of history that in 1834, at New Salem, Ill.,
> Lincoln read and circulated Volney's *Ruins* and Paine's *Age of
> Reason*, giving to both books the sincere recommendation of his
> unqualified approval. About that time or a little later he wrote
> an extensive argument against Christianity, intending to publish
> it. In this argument he contended that the Bible was not inspired
> and that Jesus Christ was not the son of God. He read this com-
> pilation of his views to numerous friends, and on one occasion
> when he so engaged his friend and employer, Samuel Hill,
> snatched the manuscript from the author's hands and threw it
> into the stove, where it was quickly consumed. A Springfield
> friend said of him in 1838, "Lincoln was enthusiastic in his Infi-
> delity." John T. Stuart, who was his first law partner, declares:
> "Lincoln was an avowed and open Infidel. He went further
> against Christian belief than any man I ever heard. He always
> denied that Jesus was the Christ of God." David Davis stated
> that "Lincoln had absolutely no faith in the Christian sense of
> the term."
>
> These authorities ought to be conclusive, but there is
> further testimony. This latter is important as explanatory of
> Lincoln's frequent allusions in his Presidential messages and
> proclamations to the Supreme Being. To the simplicity of his
> nature there was added a poetic temperament. He was fond of
> effective imagery, and his references to the Deity are due to the
> instinct of the poet. After his death Mrs. Lincoln said: "Mr.
> Lincoln had no faith and no hope in the usual acceptation of
> those words. He never joined a church." She denominates what

has been mistaken for his expressions of religious sentiment as "a kind of poetry in his nature," adding "he was never a Christian." Herndon, who was his latest law partner and biographer, is even more explicit. He says: "No man had a stronger or firmer faith in Providence – God – than Mr. Lincoln, but the continued use by him late in life of the word "God" must not be interpreted to mean that he believed in a personal God. In 1854 he asked me to erase the word "God" from a speech which I had written and read to him for criticism, because my language indicated a personal God, whereas he insisted no such personality ever existed.

So it must be accepted as final by every reasonable mind that in religion Mr. Lincoln was a skeptic. But above all things he was not a hypocrite or pretender. He was a plain man, rugged and earnest, and he pretended to be nothing more. He believed in humanity, and he was incapable of Phariseeism. He had great respect for the feelings and convictions of others, but he was not a sniveler. He was honest and he was sincere, and taking him simply for what he was, we are not likely soon to see his like again.

Manford's Magazine

There are two Christian publications that have had the fairness to admit the truth respecting Lincoln's belief. *Manford's Magazine,* a religious periodical published in Chicago, in its issue for January, 1869, contained the following:

> That Mr. Lincoln was a believer in the Christian religion, as understood by the so-called orthodox sects of the day, I am compelled most emphatically to deny; that is, if I put faith in the statements of his most intimate friends in this city [Springfield]. All of them with whom I have conversed on this subject, agree in indorsing the statements of Mr. Herndon. Indeed, many of them unreservedly call him an Infidel.
>
> The evidence on this subject is sufficient, the writer says, to place the name of Lincoln by the side of Franklin, Washington, Jefferson, and [Ethan] Allen, of Revolutionary notoriety, as Rationalists; besides being in company with D'Alembert, the great mathematician, Diderot, the geometrician, poet, and metaphysician;

also with Voltaire, Hume, Gibbon, and Darwin.

Referring to the Infidel book, written by Lincoln, the writer says:

> This work was subsequently thrown in Mr. Lincoln's face while he was stumping this district for Congress against the celebrated Methodist preacher, Rev. Peter Cartwright. But Mr. Lincoln never publicly or privately denied its authorship, or the sentiments expressed therein. Nor was he known to change his religious views any, to the latest period of his life.

The article concludes with these truthful words: "Mr. Lincoln was too good a man to be a Pharisee; too great a man to be a sectarian; and too charitable a man to be a bigot."

Herald and Review

This work, in an abridged form, originally appeared in the *Truth Seeker* in 1889 and 1890. After its appearance, the Adventist *Herald and Review,* one of the fairest and most ably conducted religious journals in this country, said:

> The *Truth Seeker* has just concluded the publication of a series of fifteen contributed articles designed to prove that Abraham Lincoln, instead of being a Christian, as has been most strongly claimed by some, was a Freethinker. The testimony seems conclusive. . . . The majority of the great men of the world have always rejected Christ, and, according to the Scriptures, they always will; and the efforts of Christians to make it appear that certain great men who never professed Christianity were in reality Christians, is simply saying that Christianity cannot stand on its merits, but must have the support of great names to entitle it to favorable consideration.

Chambers's Encyclopedia

Alden's American Edition of *Chambers's Encyclopedia,* one of the most popular as well as one of the most reliable of encyclopedias, says:

> He [Lincoln] was never a member of a church; he is
> believed to have had philosophical doubts of the divinity of Christ,
> and of the inspiration of the Scriptures, as these are commonly
> stated in the system of doctrines called evangelical. In early life
> he read Yolney and Paine, and wrote an essay in which he agreed
> with their conclusions. Of modern thinkers he was thought to agree
> nearest with Theodore Parker.[1]

Encyclopedia Britannica

By whom the article on Lincoln in *Chambers's Encyclopedia* was written, whether by one of Lincoln's personal friends,
or by a stranger, I know not. The article in the *Britannica* was
written by his private secretary, Colonel Nicolay. In this article
his religion is briefly summed up in the following words: "His
[Lincoln's] nature was deeply religious, but he belonged to no
denomination; he had faith in the eternal justice and boundless
mercy of Providence; and made the Golden Rule of Christ his
practical creed."[2]

This statement at first glance presents a Christian appearance, and the reader is liable to infer that the writer aims to state
that Lincoln was a Christian. But he does not. He aims to state in
the least offensive manner possible that he was not that he was
simply a Deist. A person may have a "deeply religious" nature,
and not be a Christian. He may have "faith in the eternal justice
and boundless mercy of Providence," and yet have no faith whatever in Christianity. He may make "the Golden Rule of Christ [or
Confucius] his practical creed," and at the same time wholly
reject the dogma of Christ's divinity. The above statement is
substantially true as applied to Lincoln, and it would be equally
true if applied to that prince of Infidels, Thomas Paine. His nature was deeply religious; he had faith in the justice and mercy

---

1. Art. "Lincoln, Abraham."
2. Am. Ed., vol. xiv, p. 669.

of Providence; and he, too, made the Golden Rule his practical creed.

People's Library of Information

Mrs. Lincoln was nominally a Presbyterian, and frequently, though not regularly, attended the Rev. Dr. Gurley's church in Washington. Lincoln usually accompanied her, not because he derived any pleasure or benefit from the services, but because he believed it to be a duty he owed to his wife who, in turn, generally accompanied him when he went to his church, the theater. *The People's Library of Information* contains the following relative to his church attendance:

> Lincoln attended service once a day. He seemed always to be in agony while in church. . . . His pastor, Dr. Gurley, had the gift of continuance, and the President writhed and squirmed and gave unmistakable evidence of the torture he endured.

The World's Sages

In *The World's Sages*, Mr. Bennett writes as follows concerning Lincoln's belief:

> Upon the subject of religious belief there is some diversity of claims. All his friends and acquaintances readily admit that in early manhood and middle age he was an unbeliever, or a Deist. In fact, he wrote a book or pamphlet vindicating this view. His most intimate friends that knew him best, claim that his opinions underwent no change in this respect; while a certain number of Christians have, since his death, undertaken to make out that he had become a convert to Christianity. . . .
>
> When the contradictory character of the evidence is taken into consideration, together with the fact that his nearest and most intimate friends would be most likely the ones to know of Mr. Lincoln's change, had any such taken place, the incredibility of the asserted change is easily appreciated.[3]

---

3. *World's Sages*, pp. 773, 774.

The Every-Day Life of Lincoln

In the Emancipation Proclamation appears the following paragraph, which contains the only allusion to Deity to be found in this immortal document: "And upon this act, sincerely believed to be an act of justice, warranted by the Constitution, upon military necessity, I invoke the considerate judgment of mankind and the gracious favor of Almighty God." The appearance of the above paragraph in the Proclamation is thus accounted for in Francis F. Brown's *Every-Day Life of Lincoln*, and agrees with Judge Usher's and Chief Justice Chase's account of it:

> It is stated that Mr. Lincoln gave the most earnest study to the composition of the Emancipation Proclamation. He realized, as he afterward said, that the Proclamation was the central act of his administration, and the great event of the Nineteenth Century. When the document was completed, a printed copy of it was placed in the hands of each member of the Cabinet, and criticisms and suggestions were invited. Mr. Chase remarked: "This paper is of the utmost importance, greater than any state paper ever made by this Government. A paper of so much importance, and involving the liberties of so many people, ought, I think, to make some reference to Deity. I do not observe anything of the kind in it."[4]

The amendment suggested was allowed by the President, and Mr. Chase requested to supply the words he desired to be inserted. The paragraph quoted was accordingly prepared by him and included in the Proclamation. This fact is also admitted by Holland in his *Life of Lincoln*.[5]

Hon. Jesse W. Weik

Judge Weik, of Greencastle, Ind., who was associated with Mr. Herndon in the preparation of his *Life of Lincoln*, in a lecture

---

4. *Every-Day Life of Lincoln*, pp. 549, 550.
5. *Life of Lincoln*, p. 401.

on "Lincoln's Boyhood and Early Manhood," delivered in Plymouth Church, Indianapolis, Feb. 4, 1891, said: "As a young man he sat back of the country store stove and said the Bible was not inspired, and Christ was not the Son of God."[6]

Charles Wallace French

One of the last biographies of Lincoln that has appeared is *Abraham Lincoln, The Liberator*, written by Charles W. French. After citing with approval some of Mr. Herndon's statements regarding Lincoln's belief, Mr. French says: "The world was his [Lincoln's] church. His sermons were preached in kindly words and merciful deeds."[7]

Cyrus O. Poole

I quote next from a monograph on "The Religious Convictions of Abraham Lincoln," written by Cyrus O. Poole. Referring to Arnold's and Holland's biographies of Lincoln, Mr. Poole says:

> Most sectarians now think, write, and act as if they had a copyright to apply "Christian" to everything good and God-like about this President; yet no one presumed to call him a Christian until after his death.
>
> It may be a soul-saving process like the ancient one of Pope Gregory in the sixth century. It is related that one day he was meditating on an anecdote of the Pagan Emperor Tragan's having turned back, when at the head of his legions on his way to battle, to render justice to a poor widow who flung herself at his horse's feet. It seemed to Gregory that the soul of a prince so good could not be forever lost, Pagan though he was; and he prayed for him, till a voice declared Tragan to have been saved through his intercession. And thus, through the prayer of a Christian Pope, a pagan of the first, was materialized into a Christian in the sixth century, and was, of course, transferred from hell to heaven. Now behold how a modern politician [Arnold] can play

6. *Indianapolis News,* Feb. 5, 1891.

7. *Abraham Lincoln, The Liberator*, p. 91.

theologian in Christianizing Abraham Lincoln.

There is now hope for Benjamin Franklin, John Adams, and Thomas Jefferson, as well as the chieftains, Red Jacket, Tecumseh, and Black Hawk.

Respecting Lincoln's message to his dying father, Mr. Poole, himself a firm believer in the doctrine of immortality, says: "This prophetic affirmation of a continued existence, is the only written evidence of his views on this momentous question that can be found."

In addition to the above, I cull from the same work the following brief extracts:

He lived in a remarkably formative and progressive period, and was in all matters fully abreast with his time. As a truthful thinker, he greatly excelled any of the statesmen of his day. . . .

Lincoln, like Socrates, was a man so natural, so thoughtful, rational, and sagacious, that he clearly saw that the popular traditional theology of his day and age was not religion.

A Citizen of Springfield

A gentleman residing in Springfield, Ill., who was intimately acquainted with Lincoln from the time he located in that city up to the time he removed to Washington – a period of nearly twenty-five years – in a letter dated Aug. 20, 1887, writes as follows:

I will say in regard to Mr. Lincoln's religious views that he was not orthodox in his belief, unless he changed after he left Springfield. He was heterodox – did not believe in the divinity of Christ – in short, was a Freethinker. Now I do not want to be brought into public notice in this matter.

In deference to this writer's request, his name is omitted, and this omission destroys, to a great extent, the value of his testimony. It is inserted not because it adds any particular weight to the evidence already adduced, but as a specimen of a very large amount of evidence of the same character that must be withheld simply because the persons writing or interviewed shrink from publicity. A chapter, yes, a volume, of this anonymous testimony might be given. At least a hundred personal friends of Lincoln, living in and about Springfield, privately and confidentially assert that he was an Infidel, but will not permit their names to be used. Twenty years ago a majority of them would not have objected to their statements being published; but the relentless war waged by the church against those who have publicly certified to the facts has sealed their lips.

Henry Walker

I now present to the reader another citizen of Springfield, one who is not afraid to publicly express an honest opinion. Mr. Henry Walker, who has resided in that city for many years, writes as follows concerning Lincoln's religious belief:

> After inquiring of those who were intimate and familiar with him, I arrive at the conclusion that he was a Deist. . . .
> There is a rumor current here that he once wrote an anti-Christian pamphlet, but his friends persuaded him not to publish it.

Mr. Walker was not personally acquainted with Lincoln. His conclusion is simply based upon the information obtained from those who were acquainted with him. His statement, like the preceding one, is introduced not so much because of any especial value attaching to it as mere testimony, but because it fairly represents the common sentiment of those who have investigated this subject, and particularly those who are on familiar terms with Lincoln's old associates in Illinois. The knowledge of our anonymous witness was shared by Dr. Smith, Mr. Arnold, and Mr. Edwards; the opinion expressed by Mr. Walker was the opinion privately entertained by Dr. Holland, it *is* the opinion privately entertained by Mr. Bateman, yes, and unquestionably the opinion privately entertained by Mr. Reed himself.

William Bissett

An article on Lincoln's religion written by Mr. Wm. Bissett, of Santa Ana, Calif., and recently published in the *Truth Seeker,* contains some evidence that deserves to be recorded. Mr. Bissett narrates the following:

> In the Spring of 1859 we moved into Livingston county, Mo., near Chillicothe. We at once became acquainted with a man by the name of William Jeeter. Mr. Jeeter was a native of Kentucky, and if I mistake not, was born and raised in the same part of the country that Mr. Lincoln was – but about that I am not sure. Mr. Jeeter told me that Lincoln and himself settled in Illinois when they were young men, and boarded together for a number of years. He says he knew every act of Lincoln's life up to the time he (Jeeter) left Illinois, a few years before Mr. Lincoln's nomination for the Presidency. I was helping Jeeter build a house for himself when we received the news of Mr. Lincoln's nomination; that is why we came to steak so particularly about him. Mr. Jeeter told me that Mr. Lincoln was not a believer in the Christian religion; that is, he did not believe the Bible was an inspired work, nor that Jesus Christ was the son of God. "Nevertheless," said Mr. Jeeter, "he was one of the most honest men I ever knew. If I had a million dollars I wouldn't be afraid to trust it to Lincoln without the scratch of a pen, I know the man so well." Mr. Jeeter was a strong believer in the Christian religion and a member of the Cumberland Presbyterian church, and a very fine and reliable man.

Frederick Heath

The following is from an article on Lincoln by Mr. Frederick Heath, of Milwaukee, Wis.:

> Two years ago I was associated with Major Geo. H. Norris, a wealthy orange-grower of Florida, in that state, and was in a degree his *confidant.* In earlier years, while a lawyer in Illinois, Major Norris (he was at one time mayor of Ottawa, Ill.) was quite closely associated with Mr. Lincoln, and he gave me to understand that Mr. Lincoln was an extreme skeptic. They were thrown to-

gether a good deal at Springfield, where they were trying cases before the supreme court. Lincoln would frequently keep them from sleep by his stories and arguments, and frequently spoke of religious matters in a way that showed he was convinced of the delusion of faith. I wish I could quote the Major's words as to Lincoln's remarks on religion, but will not venture to frame them, as this is a subject that demands truth and exactness.

Rev. Edward Eggleston

When Lincoln went to New York in the winter of 1860, to deliver his Cooper Institute address, he had occasion to remain over Sunday in that city. At the suggestion of a friend, he visited the famous Five Points, and attended a Sunday-school where the spawn of New York's worst inhabitants to the number of several hundred were assembled. Importuned for a speech, he made a few remarks to the children, and the fact was published in the papers. The idea of this Infidel politician addressing a Sunday-school was so ludicrous that it caused much merriment among his friends at Springfield. When he returned home one of them, probably Colonel Matheny, called on him to learn what it all meant. The conversation that followed, including Lincoln's explanation of the affair, is thus related by the noted preacher and author, Edward Eggleston:

> He started for "Old Abe's" office; but bursting open the door impulsively, found a stranger in conversation with Mr. Lincoln. He turned to retrace his steps, when Lincoln called out, "Jim! What do you want?"
> "Nothing."
> "Yes, you do; come back."
> After some entreaty Jim approached Mr. Lincoln, and remarked, with a twinkle in his eye, "Well Abe, I see you have been making a speech to Sunday-school children. What's the matter?"
> "Sit down, Jim, and I'll tell you all about it." And with that Lincoln put his feet on the stove and began: "When Sunday morning came, I didn't know exactly what to do. Washburne asked me where I was going. I told him I had nowhere to go; and he

proposed to take me down to the Five Points Sunday-school, to show me something worth seeing. I was very much interested by what I saw. Presently, Mr. Pease came up and spoke to Mr. Washburne, who introduced me. Mr. Pease wanted us to speak. Washburne spoke, and then I was urged to speak. I told them I did not know anything about talking to Sunday-schools, but Mr. Pease said many of the children were friendless and homeless, and that a few words would do them good. Washburne said I must talk. And so I rose to speak; but I tell you, Jim, I didn't know what to say. I remembered that Mr. Pease said that they were homeless and friendless, and I thought of the time when I had been pinched by terrible poverty. And so I told them that I had been poor; that I remembered when my toes stuck out through my broken shoes in winter; when my arms were out at the elbows; when I shivered with the cold. And I told them there was only one rule. That was, always do the very best you can. I told them that I had always tried to do the very best I could; and that, if they would follow that rule, they would get along somehow. That was about what I said."[8]

The foregoing is significant. Lincoln was not an advocate of Sunday-schools. He had probably never visited one before. As generally conducted, he regarded them as simply nurseries of superstition. He could not indorse the religious ideas taught in them, and he was not there that day to antagonize them. As a consequence, this ready talker – this man who had been making speeches all his life – was, for the first time, at a loss to know what to say. He could not talk to them about the Bible – he could not tell them that "it is the best gift which God has given to man" – that "all the good from the Savior of the world is communicated to us through this book" – that "but for this book we could not know right from wrong" – he could not tell them how Jesus had died for little children, and all this, because he did not believe it. But he obeyed his own life-long rule, did the best he could under the embarrassing circumstances, and gave them a little wholesome advice entirely free from the usual Sunday-school cant.

---

8. *Every-Day Life of Lincoln*, pp. 322, 323.

Rev. Robert Collyer

Robert Collyer states that Lincoln, just before he was elected President, visited the office of the *Chicago Tribune,* and picking up a volume of Theodore Parker's writings, turned to Dr. Bay and remarked: "I think that I stand about where that man stands."

Allen Thorndike Rice

The lamented Allen Thorndike Rice, whose brilliant editorial management of the *North American Review* has placed this periodical in the front rank of American magazines, in his Introduction to the *Reminiscences of Lincoln*, says:

> The Western settlers had no respect for English traditions, whether of Church or of State. Accustomed all their lives to grapple with nature face to face, they thought and they spoke, with all the boldness of unrestrained sincerity, on every topic of human interest or of sacred memory, without the slightest recognition of any right of external authority to impose restrictions, or even to be heard in protest against their intellectual independence. As their life developed the utmost independence of creed and individuality, he whose originality was the most fearless and self-contained was chief among them. Among such a people, blood of their blood and bone of their bone, differing from them only in stature, Abraham Lincoln arose to rule the American people with a more than kingly power, and received from them a more than feudal loyalty.

So eager is the church for proofs of Lincoln's piety that the most incredible anonymous story in support of this claim is readily accepted and published by the religious press as authentic history. By this means the masses have gradually come to regard Lincoln as a devout Christian. It is evident that Mr. Rice had these fabulous tales in mind when he wrote the following:

> Story after story and trait after trait, as varying in value as in authenticity, has been added to the Lincolniana, until at

last the name of the great war President has come to be a bio-graphic lodestone, attracting without distinction or discrimina-tion both the true and the false.

Robert C. Adams

The noted author, Capt. Robert C. Adams, of Montreal, Can., says:

It is significant that in political revolution it is the Free-thinker who is usually the leader. Franklin, Paine, Jefferson, Washington, were the chief founders of the American Republic, and *Lincoln presided at its second birth.* Mazzini and Garibaldi are the heroes of United Italy; Rousseau, Votaire, and Victor Hugo have been the chief inspirers of Democratic France.

Theodore Stanton

In the *Westminster Review* for September, 1891, Mr. Stanton had an article discussing the moral character and reli-gious belief of Abraham Lincoln. Of his religious belief, he says:

If Lincoln had lived and died an obscure Springfield lawyer and politician he would unquestionably have been classed by his neighbors among Freethinkers. But, as is customary with the church, whether Roman Catholic or Protestant, when Lincoln became one of the great of the world an attempt was made to claim him. In trying to arrive at a correct comprehension of Lincoln's theology this fact should be borne in mind in sifting the testimony.

Another very important warping influence which should not be lost sight of was Lincoln's early ambition for political preferment. Now, the shrewd American politician with an elastic conscience joins some church, and is always seen on Sunday in the front pews. But the shrewd politician who has not an elastic conscience – and this was Lincoln's case – simply keeps mum on his religious views, or, when he must touch on the subject, deals only in platitudes.

After citing the testimony of many of Lincoln's friend, Mr. Stanton concludes: "A man about whose theology such things can be said is of course far removed from orthodoxy. It may even be questioned whether he is a Theist, whether he is a Deist. That he is a Freethinker is evident; that he is an Agnostic is probable."

Geo. M. McCrie

In the *Open Court* for Nov. 26, 1891, Mr. McCrie contributes an article on "What Was Abraham Lincoln's Creed?" Concerning Lincoln's allusions to God, he says:

> A Deity thus shelved or not shelved, according to the dictates of political expediency, or of individual opinion as to the "propriety" of either course is no Deity at all. He is as fictional as the "John Doe" or "Richard Roe" of a legal writ, and anyone making use of such a creation – the puppet, not the parent, of his own Egoity – is supposed to know with what he is dealing. Orthodox religionism may well despair of Abraham Lincoln as of George Washington, Benjamin Franklin, or President Jefferson.

Gen. M. M. Trumbull

Gen. Trumbull, of Chicago, in the *Open Court of* Dec. 3, 1891, writes:

> The religion that begs the patronage of presidents doubts its own theology, for the true God needs not the favor of men. . . . Some of his [Lincoln's] tributes to Deity are merely rhetorical emphasis, but others were not. Cicero often swore "By Hercules," as in the oration against Catiline, although he believed no more in Hercules than Abraham Lincoln believed in any church-made God.

Rev. David Swing, D.D.

In a sermon on "Washington and Lincoln," the most eminent and popular divine of Chicago, Dr. Swing said:

It is often lamented by the churchmen that Washington and Lincoln possessed little religion except that found in the word "God." All that can here be affirmed is that what the religion of those two men lacked in theological details it made up in greatness. Their minds were born with a love of great principles. . . . There are few instances in which a mind great enough to reach great principles in politics has been satisfied with a fanatical religion. . . . It must not be asked for Washington and Lincoln that, having reached greatness in political principles, they should have loved littleness in piety.

Rev. Jenkin Lloyd Jones

The Rev. J. Lloyd Jones, one of Chicago's most eloquent divines, in a sermon preached in All Souls Church, Dec. 9, 1888, gave utterance to the following:

Are there not thousands who have loved virtue who did not accept Jesus Christ in any supernatural or miraculous fashion, who if they knew of him at all knew of him only as the Nazarene peasant – the man Jesus? Such was Abraham Lincoln, the tender prophet of the gospel of good will upon earth; Charles Sumner, the great apostle of human liberty; Gerrit Smith, the St. John of political reform; William Ellery Channing, our sainted preacher; Theodore Parker, the American Luther, hurling his defiance at the devils of bigotry; John Stuart Mill and Harriet Martineau – yes, to take an extreme case, the genial and over-satirical Robert G. Ingersoll, are among those who love goodness and foster nobility, though they have no clear vision into futurity and confess no other lordship in him of Nazareth save the dignity of aim and tenderness of life.

Rev. John W. Chadwick

In an address delivered in Tremont Temple, Boston, May 30, 1872, the Rev. John W. Chadwick, of Brooklyn, N.Y., referring to the proposed religious amendment to the Constitution of the United States, said:

Of the six men who have done most to make America the wonder and the joy she is to all of us, not one could be the citizen of a government so constituted; for Washington and Franklin and Jefferson, certainly the three mightiest leaders in our early history, were heretics in their day, Deists, as men called them; and Garrison and Lincoln and Sumner, certainly the three mightiest in these later times, would all be disfranchised by the proposed amendment. . . .

Lincoln could not have taken the oath of office had such a clause been in the Constitution.

CHAPTER FOURTEEN:
Evidence Gathered From Lincoln's Letters, Speeches, and Conversations
☆　☆　☆　☆

The Bible and Christianity – Christ's Divinity – Future Rewards
and Punishments – Freedom of Mind – Fatalism – Providence
Lines in Copy-book – Parker – Paine – Opposition of Church
Clerical Officiousness Rebuked – Irreverent Jokes – Profanity
Temperance Reform – Indorsement of Lord Bolingbroke's
Writings – Golden Rule

The testimony of one hundred witnesses will now be supplemented by evidence from the tongue and pen of Lincoln himself. The greater portion of what he wrote and uttered against Christianity has perished; but enough has been preserved to demonstrate, even in the absence of other evidence, that he was not a Christian. From his letters, speeches, and recorded conversations, the following radical sentiments have been extracted.

Notwithstanding the efforts of Holland and Bateman to prove that Lincoln was a believer in Christianity, it is admitted that in his conversation with Bateman, he said: "I am not a Christian."[1]

When his Christian friends at Petersburg interfered to prevent his proposed duel with Shields, and told him that it was contrary to the teachings of the Bible and Christianity, he remarked: "The Bible is not my book, nor Christianity my profession."[2]

---

1. Holland's *Life of Lincoln*, pp. 236, 237.
2. Letter of W. Perkins.

191

While at Washington, in a letter to his old friend, Judge Wakefield, written in 1862, in answer to inquiries respecting his belief and the expressed hope that he had become convinced of the truth of Christianity, he replied as follows:

> My earlier views of the unsoundness of the Christian scheme of salvation and the human origin of the Scriptures have become clearer and stronger with advancing years and I see no reason for thinking I shall ever change them.

In a discussion touching upon the paternity of Jesus, he said: "There must have been sexual intercourse between man and woman, and not between God and his daughter."

The above words were uttered in the presence of Green Caruthers and Mr. W. A. Browning, of Springfield.

Lincoln contended that Jesus was either the son of Joseph and Mary, or the illegitimate son of Mary.

In a conversation with his friend, Mr. E. H. Wood, of Springfield, concerning the doctrine of endless punishment, he said: "There is no hell."

In regard to this subject, he often observed: "If God be a just God, all will be saved or none."[3]

The orthodox idea of God – a God that creates poor, fallible beings, and then forever damns them for failing to believe what it is impossible for them to believe – he abhorred. The Golden Rule was his moral standard, and by this standard he measured not only the conduct of man, but of God himself. Like the irrepressible Dr. T.L. Brown, he wanted God to damn others as he would be damned himself." He delighted to repeat the epitaph of the old Kickapoo Indian, Johnnie Kongapod:

> Here lies poor Johnnie Kongapod;
> Have mercy on him, gracious God,
> As he would do if he were God
> And you were Johnnie Kongapod.

---

3. *Manford's Magazine.*

Lincoln thought that God ought at least to be as merciful as a respectable savage.

Many contend that the doctrine of future rewards and punishments, even if untrue, has a restraining influence upon the masses of mankind. That Lincoln did not share this fallacious opinion, is shown by the following extract from an address delivered in Springfield in 1842:

> Pleasures to be enjoyed, or pains to be endured, after we shall be dead and gone, are but little regarded. . . . There is something so ludicrous, in promises of good, or threats of evil, a great way off, as to render the whole subject with which they are connected, easily turned into ridicule. "Better lay down that spade you're stealing, Paddy – if you don't, you'll pay for it at the Day of Judgment." "Be the powers, if ye'll credit me so long I'll take another."[4]

Commenting upon the question of one's returning and communicating with his friends after death, he observed: "It is a doubtful question whether we ever get anywhere to get back."[5]

He did not believe in the freedom of the will. An observation which he repeatedly made was the following: No man has a freedom of mind."[6]

His fatalistic notions are confirmed by his own words: "I have all my life been a fatalist. What is to be will be; or, rather, I have found all my life, as Hamlet says:

> 'There's a divinity that shaped our ends,
> Rough-hew them how we will.'"[7]

The following was a favorite maxim with him: "What is to be will be, and no prayers of ours can arrest the decree."[8]

---

4. *Lincoln Memorial Album*, p. 91.

5. Statement of E. H. Wood.

6. Testimony of W. H. Herndon.

7. *Every-Day Life of Lincoln*, p 198.

8. Statement of Mrs. Lincoln.

In a speech on Kansas, delivered in 1856, he used the following words in regard to Providence: "Friends, I agree with you in Providence; but I believe in the Providence of the most men, the largest purse, and the longest cannon."[9]

The writer has in his possession, among others of Lincoln's papers, a leaf from his copybook, tattered and yellow from age, on which, seventy years ago, Lincoln, a school-boy of fourteen, wrote the following characteristic lines:

"Abraham Lincoln, his hand and pen;
He will be good, but God knows when."

If by *good* he meant *pious,* the prophecy was never fulfilled. But a short time before he was elected Presidents, he said to Dr. Ray: "I think that I stand about where that man [Theodore Parker] stands."[10]

The author whose writings exerted the greatest influence upon Lincoln's mind, in a theological way, was Thomas Paine. Ah! that potential *Age of Reason*! Criticise it as you may, no one ever yet carefully perused its pages and then honestly affirmed that the Bible is the infallible word of God. Herndon and others declare that Paine was a part of Lincoln from 1834 till his death. To a friend he said: "I never tire of reading Paine."[11]

In the later years of his life, when the subject of religion was mentioned, with a knowing smile, he was wont to remark: "It will not do to investigate the subject of religion too closely, as it is apt to lead to Infidelity."[12]

It has been stated that Lincoln was opposed in his political campaigns on account of his disbelief. This is confirmed by a letter he wrote to Martin M. Morris, of Petersburg, Ill., March 26, 1843. In this letter, he says:

---

9. *Lincoln's Speeches*, p. 140.
10. Statement of Rev. Robert Collyer.
11. Statement of James Tuttle.
12. *Manford's Magazine.*

There was, too, the strangest combination of church influence against me. Baker is a Campbellite; and therefore, as I suppose, with few exceptions, got all that church. My wife has some relatives in the Presbyterian churches, and some with the Episcopal churches; and therefore, wherever it would tell, I was set down as either the one or the other, while it was everywhere contended that no Christian ought to go for me, because I belonged to no church – was suspected of being a Deist. . . . Those influences levied a tax of a considerable per cent. upon my strength throughout the religious controversy.[13]

He never changed his opinions, and the church never ceased to oppose him. In the Bateman interview, seventeen years later, he was compelled to note its relentless intolerance:

Here are twenty-three ministers of different denominations, and all of them are against me but three; and here are a great many prominent members of the churches, a very large majority of whom are against me.[14]

For thirty years the church endeavored to crush Lincoln, but when, in spite of her malignant opposition, he achieved a glorious immortality, this same church, to hide the mediocrity of her devotees, attempts to steal his deathless name.

In a speech delivered in Springfield, in 1857, alluding to the negro, he said: "All the powers of the earth seem rapidly combining against him. Mammon is after him, and the theology of the day is fast joining in the cry."[15]

The theology of the day was orthodox Christianity. "In this sentence," says Mr. Herndon, "he intended to hit Christianity a left-handed blow, and a hard one."

In his Second Inaugural address, referring to the contending Christian elements in the Civil War, he says: "Both read the same Bible and pray to the same God, and each invokes his aid

---

13. Lamon's *Life of Lincoln*, p. 271.
14. Holland's *Life of Lincoln*, p. 236.
15. *Lincoln Memorial Album*, p. 100.

against the other." What a commentary upon the hypocritical assumption that Christians possess an infallible moral standard, is contained in the above words!

The *Lincoln Memorial Album* pretends to give the Second Inaugural complete, but omits the words quoted. As this address comes almost immediately after his reputed speech to the "Illinois clergyman," the editor probably noticed a lack of harmony between the two, and thought that the retention of these heretical words would cast suspicion upon the genuineness of that remarkable confession. The *Memorial Album* is a meritorious work, but had Mr. Oldroyd manifested as great a desire to present the genuine utterances of Lincoln as the apocryphal, its value would have been enhanced. The unmutilated version of the last Inaugural may be found in Holland's *Life of Lincoln;*[16] Arnold's *Life of Lincoln;*[17] Arnold's *Lincoln and Slavery;*[18] and *The Every-Day Life of Lincoln.*[19]

No President, probably, was ever so much annoyed by the clergy as Lincoln. The war produced an increased religious fervor, and theological tramps innumerable, usually labeled "D.D.," visited the White House, each with a mission to perform and a precious morsel of advice to offer. In the following caustic words, he expresses his contempt for their officiousness:

> I am approached with the most opposite opinions and advice, and by religious men who are certain they represent the Divine will. . . . I hope it will not be irreverent in me to say, that if it be probable that God would reveal his will to others, on a point so connected with my duty, it might be supposed he would reveal it directly to me.[20]

Equally pertinent, and, indeed, similar was his language

---

16. Holland's *Life of Lincoln*, pp. 503, 504.

17. Arnold's *Life of Lincoln*, pp. 403, 404.

18. Arnold's *Lincoln and Slavery*, pp. 625-627.

19. *The Every-Day Life of Lincoln*, pp. 681, 682.

20. *Religious Convictions of Abraham Lincoln.*

to a pious lady, a Friend, who came as God's agent to instruct him what to do:

> I have neither time nor disposition to enter into discussion with the Friend, and end this occasion by suggesting for her consideration the question, whether, if it be true that the Lord has appointed me [she claimed that he had] to do the works she has indicated, it is not probable that he would have communicated knowledge of the fact to me as well as to her?[21]

He steadily prohibited his generals from meddling with the religious affairs of those residing within the limits of their respective departments, and at the same time counseled them not to permit the pretended sanctity of the church to shield offenders from justice.

In a letter to General Curtis, censuring the provost marshal of St. Louis for interfering with church matters, he writes: "The United States Government must not undertake to run the churches. When an individual in a church, or out of it, becomes dangerous to the public interest he must be checked."[22]

In an order relating to a church in Memphis, issued May 13, 1864, he said:

> If there be no military need for the building, leave it alone, neither putting any one in or out of it, except on finding some one preaching or practicing treason, in which case lay hands upon him, just as if he were doing the same thing in any other building.[23]

During the war his attention was called to the notoriously bad character of army chaplains. He expressed his contempt for them, and for orthodox preachers generally, by relating the following story:

---

21. *Every-Day Life of Lincoln*, pp. 536, 537.
22. Nicolay and Hay's *Life of Lincoln*.
23. *Ibid.*

Once, in Springfield, I was going off on a short journey, and reached the depot a little ahead of time. Leaning against the fence just outside the depot was a little darky boy, whom I knew, named Dick, busily digging with his toe in a mud-puddle. As I came up. I said, "Dick, what are you about?"

"Making a church," said he.

"A church?" said I; "what do you mean?"

"Why, yes," said Dick, pointing with his toe, "don't you see? there is the shape of it – there's the steps and front door here's the pews, where the folks set and there's the pulpit."

"Yes, I see," said I, "but why don't you make a minister?"

"Laws," answered Dick, with a grin, "I hain't got *mud* enough."[24]

The most highly aristocratic church in Washington is St. John's Episcopal church. So very aristocratic is it that applicants for membership deem it necessary to give references respecting their social standing in the community. The *New York Star* relates the following joke which Lincoln once perpetrated at the expense of this church:

One day during the war a young officer called on him to secure an appointment in the army, and brought with him letters of recommendation signed by the F.F.V.'s in the District of Columbia. There had been no application for office before President Lincoln so strongly supported by the aristocracy, and, turning to the young man, he said he would give him the appointment and handed him back the papers.

"Don't you want to place the papers on file?" asked the office-seeker.

"I supposed that was the custom."

"Yes, that is the custom," said President Lincoln, "but you had better take them with you, as you might want to join St. John's church."

Did Lincoln ever use profane language? If he did, this

---

24. *Anecdotes of Lincoln*, p. 86.

fact will afford no evidence to Freethinkers that he was a disbeliever in Christianity. Freethinkers are as free from this vice, if vice it be, as Christians. Very pious persons, however, such as Lincoln is represented to have been by his Christian biographers, are very careful about their use of profane words. Christ commanded his followers to pray in private, and bade them swear not at all. Devout Christians usually pray in public and swear in private. Lincoln was but little addicted to profanity, but if he had occasion to use a word of this character, he did not go to his closet to use it. In a business letter to a friend, he said: "A d—d hawk-billed Yankee is here besetting me at every turn."[25]

In a letter to Speed, concerning an alleged murder case, he wrote: "Hart, the little drayman that hauled Molly home once, said it was too *damned* bad to have so much trouble and no hanging."[26]

For the sake of pleasing the "fools," he attached his signature to "the pious nonsense of Seward." With equal readiness he indorsed the profane nonsense (?) of Stanton. During the war the patriotic Lovejoy had devised a military scheme which he believed would prove beneficial to the Union cause, and obtained an order from the President for its execution. He took the order to Stanton, but all that ever resulted from it was the following spirited colloquy:

"Did Lincoln give you an order of that kind?" said Stanton.

"He did, sir."

"Then he is a d—d fool," said the irate Secretary.

"Do you mean to say the President is a d—d fool?" asked Lovejoy, in amazement.

"Yes, sir, if he gave you such an order as that."

The bewildered Illinoisan betook himself at once to the President, and related the result of his conference. "Did Stanton say I was a d—d fool?" asked Lincoln at the close of the recital.

"He did, sir, and repeated it."

---

25. Lamon's *Life of Lincoln*, p. 316.

26. *Ibid*, p. 321.

After a moment's pause, and looking up, the President said: "If Stanton said I was a d—d fool, then *I must be one,* for he is nearly always right, and generally says what he means."[27]

At a Cabinet meeting, in 1863, when a conflict between the President and Congress regarding the admission of certain representatives from loyal districts of the South, which he favored, was threatened, he turned to Secretary Chase, and exclaimed: "There it is, sir. I am to be bullied by Congress, am I? If I do I'll be d—d!"

When Lincoln visited New Orleans he attended a slave sale. A beautiful girl, almost white, was placed upon the auction block and exposed to the grossest indignities. As he turned to leave, boiling with indignation, he exclaimed: "By God, if I ever get a chance to hit that institution, I will hit it hard."[28] Thirty years later the chance came. He struck the blow a mortal one.

The following is a prayer which Lincoln, while at the White House, put into the mouth of a belated traveler who was caught in a violent thunderstorm: "O Lord, if it is all the same to you, give us a little more light and a little less noise!"[29]

Is it possible that a Christian and a Calvinist would repeat such an irreverent, not to say blasphemous, supplication? According to the Brooklyn Calvinist, God visits such supplicants with paralysis and petrifaction.

Like most Freethinkers, Lincoln was a genuine reformer. The Antislavery reform was not the only reform that enlisted his support. At an early day he espoused the Temperance cause. When the church was the ally of intemperance as it was of slavery when, to use his own words, "From the sideboard of the parson down to the ragged pocket of the houseless loafer intoxicating liquor was constantly found," he was laboring and lecturing in behalf of the Washingtonian movement. With the fervor of an enthusiast, he exclaims in true Freethought language:

---

27. *Every-Day Life of Lincoln*, pp. 483, 484.
28. Arnold's *Life of Lincoln*, Note.
29. *Six Months at the White House*, p. 49.

Happy day, when, all appetites controlled, all passions subdued, all matter subjugated, mind, all-conquering mind, shall live and move, the monarch of the world! Glorious consummation! Hail, fall *of fury! Reign of Reason, all hail!*[30]

To sumptuary laws and to the denunciatory methods so common among orthodox Christians to-day, he was, however, strenuously opposed. He says: "It is not much in the nature of man to be driven to anything; still less to be driven about that which is exclusively his own business. . . . When the conduct of men is designed to be influenced, persuasion, kind, unassuming persuasion, should ever be adopted."[31]

His nephew, Mr. Hall, informed me that Lincoln once made it cost a meddlesome clergyman, of Coles County, eighty dollars for seizing and destroying a quart of whisky, valued at twelve and a half cents, and belonging to a relative of theirs.

In this chapter I wish to present some radical thoughts, not from the pen of Lincoln himself, but which in the work from which they are taken bear unmistakable signs of his approval. Mr. D. W. C. Shattuck, an old and respected merchant of Wayland, Mich., has in his possession a book which belonged to Lincoln. Its history is as follows: Shortly after Lincoln's election to the Presidency a young man from Springfield, Ill., and a relative or intimate acquaintance of Lincoln's, came to board with Mr. Shattuck, who then resided in Kalamazoo. Looking over the contents of his trunk one day the young man picked up a book and at the same time remarked: "That book belongs to Abe Lincoln. I forgot to return it to him before leaving Springfield. It is his favorite book, and I must not fail to return it." Mr. Shattuck expressing a desire to peruse the work; it was handed to him, and the young man being soon after unexpectedly called away, it was forgotten. It proved to be a volume of the writings of Lord Bolingbroke, the great English Infidel. On a fly-leaf was the signature of Abraham Lincoln. In the work certain passages which seem to have especially impressed

30. *Lincoln Memorial Album*, p. 96.
31. *Ibid.*, pp. 86, 87.

Lincoln are marked with a pencil and in a manner peculiar to him. The following are the passages he marked, which I have copied from the book, and which evidently received his unqualified indorsement:

Abbadie says in his famous book, that the Gospel of St. Matthew is cited by Clemens Bishop of Rome, a disciple of the Apostles; that Barnabas cites it in his epistle; that Ignatius and Polycarp receive it; and that the same Fathers, that give testimony for Matthew, give it likewise for Mark. Nay, your lordship, will find, I believe, that the present Bishop of London, in his third pastoral letter, speaks to the same effect. I will not trouble you nor myself with any more instances of the same kind. Let this, which occurred to me as I was writing, suffice. It may well suffice; for I presume the fact advanced by the minister and the Bishop is a mistake. If the Fathers of the First Century do mention some passages that are agreeable to what we read in our Evangelists, will it follow that these Fathers had the same gospels before them? To say so is a manifest abuse of history, and quite inexcusable in writers that knew, or should have known, that these Fathers made use of other gospels, wherein such passages might be contained, or they might be preserved in unwritten tradition. Besides which I could almost venture to affirm that these Fathers of the First Century do not expressly name the gospels we have of Matthew, Mark, Luke, and John.

Writers of the Roman religion have attempted to show, that the text of the Holy Writ is on many accounts insufficient to be the sole criterion of orthodoxy; I apprehend too that they have shown it.

Sure I am that experience, from the first promulgation of Christianity to this hour, shows abundantly with how much ease and success the most opposite, the most extravagant, nay the most impious opinions, and the most contradictory faiths, may be founded on the same text; and plausibly defended by the same authority. Writers of the Reformed religion have erected their batteries against tradition; and the only difficulty they had to encounter in this enterprise lay in leveling and pointing their cannon so as to avoid demolishing, in one common ruin, the traditions they retain, and those they reject. Each side has been employed to weaken the cause and explode the system of his adversary; and, whilst they have been so employed, they have jointly laid their axes to the root of Christianity; for thus men will be apt to reason upon what they have advanced: "If the text has not that authenticity, clearness, and precision which are necessary to establish it as a divine and a certain rule of faith and practice; and if the tradition of the church from the first ages of it till the days of Luther and Calvin, has been corrupted itself, and has served to corrupt the faith and practice of Christians; there remains at this time no standard at all of Christianity. By consequence either this religion was not originally of divine institution, or else God has not provided effectually for preserving the genuine purity of it, and the gates of hell have prevailed, in contradiction to his promise, against the church."

I have read somewhere, perhaps in the works of St. Jerome, that this Father justifies the opinion of those who think it impossible to fix any certain chronology on that of the Bible; and this opinion will be justified still better, to the understanding of every man that considers how grossly the Jews blunder whenever they meddle with chronology.

The resurrection of letters was a fatal period; the Christian system has been attacked, and wounded too, very severely since that time.

When interrogated as to why he had never united with any church, Lincoln replied: "When you show me a church based on the Golden Rule as its only creed, then I will unite with it."

He never joined a church, because of all the Christian sects, not one could show such a creed. The Golden Rule conceding to others the same rights he claimed for himself was, however, the very cornerstone of Freethought, and hence he remained a Freethinker.

CHAPTER FIFTEEN:
Recapitulation and Conclusion
☆ ☆ ☆ ☆

Character of Christian Testimony – Summary of Evidence
Adduced in Proof of Lincoln's Unbelief – Douglas an Unbeliever
Theodore Parker's Theology – Fallacy of Claims Respecting
Lincoln's Reputed Conversion – His Invocations of Deity
His Alleged Regard for the Sabbath – The Church and Hypocrisy
Lincoln's Religion

In the prosecution of this inquiry, the testimony of one hundred and twenty witnesses has been presented. The testimony of twenty of these witnesses is to the effect that Lincoln was a Christian; the testimony of one hundred is to the effect that he was not.

Of those who have testified in support of the claim that Lincoln was a Christian, ten admit that during a part of his life he was a disbeliever in Christianity, while not one of the remaining ten disputes the fact. If he never changed his belief then he died an unbeliever. Did he change his belief and become a convert to Christianity? It devolves upon those who affirm that he did to prove it. Have they done this? They have not. Their attempts have been in every instance pitiable failures. The unreasonable and conflicting character of the testimony adduced refutes itself. When was he converted? No less than five different dates have been assigned. One witness states that it was in 1848; one, that it was in 1858; another, that it was in 1862; another, that it was in July, 1863; and still another, that it was in November, 1863.

The remarkable character of the statements recorded in Chapter One – remarkable when compared with the statements given in the preceding ten chapters, and not less remarkable when compared with each other – may be variously accounted for. A part of them are based upon a false premise, an erroneous conception of what the term *Christian* means; a portion of them are merely the expressions of beliefs unsupported by actual knowledge; while a not inconsiderable share of them are the statements of those who have knowingly and deliberately borne false witness. These witnesses comprise: 1. Those who do not know what constitutes a Christian – who confound Christianity with morality – who affirm that he was a Christian simply because he was a moral man. 2. Those who do not know what his religious views were, but who infer that he was a Christian because others have declared that he was, and because of the frequent allusions to Deity that occur in his speeches and state papers. 3. Those who know that he was not a Christian, but who believe it to be right and proper to lie for the glory of Christianity and the profit of its priests.

The testimony advanced in support of the claim of Lincoln's Christianity is, for the most part, the testimony of orthodox Christians – a majority of them orthodox clergymen. Dr. Holland, the chief of these Christian claimants, says: "The fact is a matter of history that he never exposed his own religious life to those who had no sympathy with it." This, so far as the later years of his life are concerned, is substantially true; and this very fact precludes the possibility of these orthodox witnesses being able to state from personal knowledge what his religious views were.

In refutation of this claim, I have presented the testimony of those who were nearest to Lincoln, in the confidential relations of life. I have presented the testimony of his wife, the testimony of his stepmother, the testimony of his step-sister, the testimony of his cousin, the testimony of his nephew, the testimony of his three law partners, the testimony of four members of his Cabinet, the testimony of his private secretary, the testimony of his executor, the testimony of seven of his biographers, and the testimony of many more of his most intimate friends both in Illinois and at Washington.

That he was not an orthodox Christian, as claimed, is attested by nearly all of the one hundred witnesses whose testimony has been given; that he was not in any sense of the term a Christian is proved by the testimony of a majority of them.

I affirmed that he was not religious in his youth – that he was a skeptic in Indiana. In proof of this, I have adduced the testimony of his step-mother, Sarah Lincoln; his step-sister, Matilda Moore; his cousin, Dennis F. Hanks; his nephew, John Hall; his law partner, W. H. Herndon, and his biographer, Col. Ward H. Lamon.

I affirmed that he was an Infidel or Freethinker, during the thirty years that he resided in Illinois. In support of this I have given the testimony of Colonel Lamon, W. H. Herndon, Maj. John T. Stuart, Col. James H. Matheny, Dr. C.H. Ray, W.H. Hannah, James W. Keys, Jesse W. Fell, Judge David Davis, Wm. McNeely, Mr. Lynan, Wm. G. Green, Joshua F. Speed, Green Caruthers, Squire Perkins, Judge Gillespie, John Decamp, James Gorley, Dr. Wm. Jayne, Jesse K. Dubois, Judge Logan, Leonard Swett, W. H. T. Wakefield, D.W. Wilder, Dr. B.F. Gardner, J.K. Vandemark, Judge Leachman, Orin B. Gould, Edward Butler, M. S. Gowin, J. H. Chenery, J. B. Spalding, Ezra String-ham, Col. B. G. Ingersoll, A. Jeffrey, Dr. McNeal, Charles McGrew, J.L. Morrell, Judge A. P. Norton, W. W. Perkins, H. K. Magie, James Tuttle, Leonard Volk, Col. F.S. Rutherford, E.H. Woods, Dr. J.J. Thompson, A. J. Grover, Judge Nelson, and others.

I affirmed that he did not change his belief after leaving Illinois – that he was not converted to Christianity in Washington – that he died an unbeliever. In confirmation of this I have presented the testimony of his wife, Mary Lincoln; of his private secretary, Colonel Nicolay; of his executor, Judge Davis; of his biographer, Colonel Lamon; and of his intimate associates, Geo. W. Julian, John B. Alley, Schuyler Colfax, Hugh McCulloch, A. J. Grover, Donn Piatt, Judge Nelson, and others.

Many of these witnesses simply testify to his disbelief in the Christian system as a whole without reference to his particular views concerning its individual tenets. Every statement of his unbelief as presented in the introduction has, however, been substantiated by the testimony of one or more witnesses.

That he did not believe in the Christian Deity, that, he even held Agnostic and Atheistic views, at times, is proved by the testimony of W. H. Herndon, Colonel Matheny, Judge Nelson, Jesse K. Dubois, and D. W. Wilder.

That he was an Agnostic in regard to the immortality of the soul is attested by E. H. Wood, Judge Nelson, and W. H. Herndon.

That he did not believe that the Bible is the word of God is affirmed by Colonel Lamon, John T. Stuart, Judge Matheny, W. H. Herndon; Jesse W. Fell, Dennis flanks, W. Perkins, Colonel Rutherford, and *Chambers' Encyclopedia.*

That he did not believe that Jesus Christ was the son of God is affirmed by Colonel Lamon, W. H. Herndon, Jesse W. Fell, Colonel Matheny, John T. Stuart, Jas. W. Keys, Judge Nelson, P. W. Wilder, Green Caruthers, Colonel Rutherford, Rev. J. Lloyd Jones, *Chambers' Encyclopedia*, and the *New York World.*

That he did not believe in a special creation, the statements of Mr. Herndon clearly prove.

That he accepted the theory of Evolution, so far as this theory had been developed in the *Vestiges of Creation* and other writings of his day, is attested by the same witness.

That he did not admit the possibility of miracles is confirmed by the statement of Jesse W. Fell, W. Perkins, Dennis Hanks, and Mr. Herndon.

That he rejected the Christian doctrine of total or inherent depravity, William McNeely and Jesse W. Fell affirm.

That he repudiated the doctrine of vicarious atonement is sustained by the testimony of Jesse W. Fell, Joshua F. Speed, W. Perkins, and Colonel Lamon.

That he condemned the doctrine of forgiveness for sin, General Wilder and Mr. Herndon both testify.

That he opposed the doctrine of future rewards and punishments, Wm. H. Hannah, E. H. Wood, A. Jeffrey, Jesse W. Fell, and *Manford's Magazine,* all testify.

That he denied the freedom of the will, Mr. Herndon explicitly affirms.

That he did not believe in the efficacy of prayer is fully established by the evidence of Mrs. Lincoln, Mr. Herndon, and Dr. Gardner.

That he was a disciple of Thomas Paine and Theodore Parker is shown by the evidence of Colonel Lamon, W. H. Herndon, James Tuttle, Jesse W. Fell, Dr. Ray, Robert Collyer, the *New York World,* and *Chambers' Encyclopedia.*

That he wrote a book against Christianity is sustained by the testimony of Colonel Matheny, Judge Nelson, W. H. Herndon, Colonel Lamon, J. B. Spalding, A. Jeffrey, J. H. Chenery, *Chicago Herald, Manford's Magazine,* and *Chambers' Encyclopedia.*

That Lincoln did not believe in the inspiration of the Scriptures, that he did not believe in the divinity of Christ, that he did not believe in the freedom of the will, that he did not believe in future rewards and punishments, that he did not believe in the efficacy of prayer, that he was, in short, a disbeliever in Christianity, is also attested by the evidence cited from his own recorded words.

In connection with this controversy the significance of the following facts cannot be overlooked: 1. Notwithstanding the strong temptation to credit Lincoln to the popular faith, a majority of his biographers have either declared that he was not a Christian, or have refrained from affirming that he was. 2. The secular press, fearing to offend the church, has generally been silent regarding the question. When it has ventured to express an opinion, however, it has been to concede his unbelief. 3. The leading encyclopedias, such as the *Britannica, Chambers', New American, etc.,* have either admitted that he was a Freethinker, or have made no reference to his religious belief. 4. In the *Lincoln Memorial Album* appear two hundred tributes to Lincoln, the greater portion of them from the pens of Christians. In but two of these two hundred tributes is it claimed that Lincoln was a believer in Christianity. 5. The *Reminiscences of Lincoln* contain thirty-three articles on Lincoln, written by as many distinguished men who were acquainted with him. In not a single instance in this work, is it asserted that he was a Christian. 6. In none of the leading eulogies pronounced upon his character, at the time of his demise, is it affirmed that he accepted Christ.

It is stated that during the last years of his life Lincoln held substantially the same theological opinions held by Theodore Parker. His own words are, referring to Parker: "I think that I stand about where that man stands." Where did Theodore Parker stand? The following extracts from his writings will show:

> To obtain a knowledge of duty, a man is not sent away, outside of himself, to ancient documents; for the only rule of faith and practice, the Word, is very nigh him, even in his heart, and by this Word he is to try all documents.
>
> There is no intercessor, angel, mediator, between man and God; for man can speak and God hear, each for himself. He requires no advocates to plead for men.
>
> Manly, natural religion it is not joining the church; it is not to believe in a creed, Hebrew, Christian, Catholic, Protestant, Trinitarian, Unitarian, Nothingarian. It is not to keep Sunday idle; to attend meeting; to be wet with water; to read the Bible; to offer prayers in words; to take bread and wine in the meeting-house; love a scapegoat Jesus, or any other theological claptrap.

If Lincoln was known to be a Freethinker, it may be asked why this fact was not more generally published and urged against him during the Presidential campaign of 1860. The answer is easy. His chief opponent, Douglas, was himself a Freethinker. Stephen A. Douglas, like Abraham Lincoln, died an unbeliever. Like Washington, he declined the services of a clergyman in his last hours. The following is an extract from a monograph on "The Deathbed of Douglas," published in the Boston *Budget*:

> When Stephen A. Douglas lay stricken with death at Chicago, his wife, who was a devout Roman Catholic, sent for Bishop Duggan, who asked whether he had ever been baptized according to the rites of any church. "Never," replied Mr. Douglas.
>
> "Do you desire to have mass said after the ordinances of the holy Catholic church?" inquired the Bishop.

"No, sir!" answered Douglas; "when I do I will commu-
nicate with you freely."

The Bishop withdrew, but the next day Mrs. Douglas
sent for him again, and, going to the bedside, he said: "Mr.
Douglas, you know your own condition fully, and in view of
your dissolution do you desire the ceremony of extreme unction
to be performed?"

"No!" replied the dying man, "I have no time to discuss
these things now."

The Bishop left the room, and Mr. Rhodes, who was in
attendance, said: "Do you know the clergymen of this city?"

"Nearly every one of them."

"Do you wish to have either or any of them to call to see
you to converse on religious topics?"

"No, I thank you," was the decided answer.

Among America's most eminent statesmen none probably
ever possessed a more logical mind than Lincoln. Judge Davis
says: "His mind was logical and direct." James G. Blaine says:
"His logic was severe and faultless." George S. Boutwell says:
"He takes rank with the first logicians and orators of every age."
In his funeral oration at Springfield, Bishop Simpson said:

> If you ask me on what mental characteristic his greatness
> rested, I answer, on a quick and ready perception of facts; on a
> memory unusually tenacious and retentive; and on a logical turn
> of mind, which followed sternly and unwaveringly every link
> in the chain of thought on every subject he was called to investi-
> gate.

Lincoln was once called to investigate the subject of Christianity. He "followed sternly and unwaveringly every link in the
chain of thought" suggested by this subject, and the result was its
rejection by him.

If he was subsequently converted to Christianity, it was
only after a re-examination and a thorough and exhaustive
investigation of its claims. This his friends positively state never
took place, and the circumstances associated with each and every
period assigned for his reputed conversion confirm their statements.

In 1848 he was a member of Congress, his mind absorbed with the novelties, the duties, and the aspirations that usually attend a first term in this important capacity. In 1858, and for years preceding and following, the great political questions of the day occupied his mind. He was engaged in a mortal struggle with one of the most powerful intellectual athletes of his time. He was contending with Douglas for a prize, and that prize was the Presidency. He must be ever on the alert. He must crush his antagonist or his antagonist would crush him. Think of Lincoln sitting down in the very crisis of this conflict and engaging in the study of theology! In 1862, and 1863, the other years assigned for his conversion, he was in the midst of the great Rebellion, all his thoughts and all his energies enlisted in the mighty task of saving the Union.

That Lincoln was a Freethinker in Illinois, that he was for a time a zealous propagandist of his faith, that he was instrumental in making unbelievers of many of his associates, it is useless to deny. If he was afterward converted to Christianity, his friends were ignorant of his conversion. He failed to notify them of his previous mistake and warn them of their impending danger. If it could be shown that he renounced his former views and became a Christian, this fact would be one of the most damaging arguments against Christianity that could be advanced. As a Freethinker he was one of the most tender and humane of men, ever solicitous for the welfare of his fellow-beings. Did Christianity transform him into a selfish, heartless being, who coolly disregarded even the eternal welfare of his best and dearest friends? Think of a man directing a friend to take a road which he afterwards discovers leads to certain death, and then not lifting a finger of warning to save him from destruction, when it is in his power to do so!

The Freethinker will require no other evidence to convince him that Lincoln died a disbeliever than the fact that he once fully investigated this subject and proclaimed himself an Infidel. The mere skeptic who has no settled convictions who has never examined the evidences against historical Christianity may become a sincere believer in the Christian religion. The confirmed Freethinker never can, albeit a Thomas Cooper, a Joseph Barker and a George Chainey may profess to. As Col. Thomas Wentworth Higginson happily expresses it:

> You may take the robin's egg from the nest in yonder tree, and so near is the bird to being hatched you may crack it with the edge of your nail, and the bird is free. But all your power, and all your patient fidelity, and all the mucilage and sticking plaster you can put on it, will never get that birdling back into that little egg again. So complete is the sense of satisfaction, such is the feeling of freedom, which comes from once finding yourself, not merely out of these little sectarian names, but out of the name of the larger and grander sect, which is Christianity, that you will find when the egg is once broken, the bird is free forever.

From the church steward's standpoint, there is nothing so desirable as the early conversion of one who is destined to become rich. From the evangelist's point of view, there is nothing like the deathbed repentance of one who has become great. Had the bullet of the assassin not immediately destroyed consciousness, all these stories that we have heard about Lincoln's conversion – the Edwards story, the Smith story, the Brooks story, the Willets story, the Vinton story, and the story of the Illinois clergyman – would never have been invented. Instead of these we would have the story of some domestic, or some intruding priest who saw him during his dying hours. Aaron Burr was kinder to the church than John Wilkes Booth.

But whatever the religious opinions of Lincoln were when he died, whether he had changed his belief or not, in view of the fact that he never thought enough of the church to unite with it, the frantic efforts of clergymen and church-members to claim him seem quite uncalled for, if not ridiculous.

The opinion of a writer previously quoted in this work, is that the bitter war waged against the persons who have declared that Lincoln was not a Christian arises, not from a belief that they have stated what is false, but from a consciousness that they have "demolished an empty shrine that was profitable to many, and broken a painted idol that might have served for a god." It is strange how Christians tend toward fetichism. Not satisfied with three Gods, they must canonize and deify men and make saints and demi-gods. They have already deified three Americans Washington, Grant, and Lincoln – and what is remarkable, in each instance they have selected an unbeliever – an Infidel. It is said that men have stolen the livery of heaven in which to serve the devil; but it seems hardly consistent with the pretensions of the church that she should be compelled to appropriate the bead-roll of Infidelity in order to make her appear respectable.

Lincoln's speeches and state papers contain many allusions to Deity. As Colonel Lamon observes, "These were easy, and not inconsistent with his religious notions." But it is a mistake to attribute all the Deistic expressions that appear in his state papers to him. Just how much of this was the work of his private secretaries, how much of it was "Seward's nonsense," or how much of it was suggested by Chase or other Cabinet ministers, can never be determined. It is significant, however, that in those documents of least importance, those which he would most likely leave to his secretaries or other officials to draft, these expressions are chiefly to be found. In his debates with Douglas, and his other great political speeches delivered in Illinois, he seldom refers to Deity. In his carefully prepared Cooper institute address, that model of political addresses, the name of Deity does not once occur. In his First Inaugural Address, he refers to God, and makes a complimentary reference to Christianity intended to conciliate the church and gain for his administration its support in the coming struggle with the South. One paragraph of the second Inaugural contains allusions to Deity and quotations from the Bible; but in this address he makes no recognition of Christ or Christianity. Even his quotations from the Bible are made in a guarded manner which clearly indicates that he did not believe in its divinity. In the Preliminary Proclamation of Emancipation, which was drafted by himself, the name of Deity does not appear. In the final Proclamation, an acknowledgment of God was inserted only at the urgent request of Secretary Chase. The Emancipation Proclamation, with the possible exception of the

Declaration of Independence and the Constitution of the United States, is the most important political document ever issued in America. He knew that this was the crowning act of his career, that it would place him among the immortals. In the preparation of this work he expended much thought and labor, and it was his desire that it should be free from religious verbiage. In that masterpiece of eloquence, the Gettysburg oration, the name of God occurs but once, while not the remotest reference to Christianity or even immortality appears. When we take into consideration the fact that this address was made at the dedication of a cemetery, the significance of this omission can not be overlooked. This speech was the product of Lincoln's own mind, free from the suggestions and emendations of others, and the occasion was too sacred to indulge in pious cant in which he did not believe.

The clergy parade Lincoln's recognitions of a Supreme Being as a triumphant refutation of the claim that he was an Infidel. Yet, at the same time, they do not hesitate to denounce as Infidels, Paine and Voltaire, when they know, or ought to know, that two more profound and reverential believers in God never lived and wrote than Paine and Voltaire.

If Infidelity and Atheism were synonymous terms it would be difficult to maintain that Lincoln, during the last years of his life at least, was an Infidel. But Infidelity and Atheism are not synonymous terms. An Atheist is an Infidel, but an Infidel is not necessarily an Atheist. A Presbyterian is a Christian, but all Christians are not Presbyterians. Christians themselves coined the word *Infidel,* and they have used it to denote a disbeliever in Christianity. A disbelief or denial of Christianity is not necessarily a denial of God. Christians, many of them, regard the term as odious and as carrying with it the idea of immorality, notwithstanding the most intelligent and the most highly moral class in Christendom are these so-called Infidels. "Who are to-day's Infidels?" says the Rev. William Channing Gannett. He answers: "Very many of the brightest minds, the warmest hearts, the most loyal consciences, the most zealous seekers after God, the most honest tellers of what they find – yes, and the most successful finders. Infidels to what are they? Not to morality: Infidels to morality are too wise to train with them."

It is not claimed that Lincoln was wholly free from a belief in the supernatural. He possessed in some respects a simple, childlike nature, and carried with him through life some of the superstitions of childhood. But the dogmas of Christianity were not among them; these he had examined and discarded.

As a proof of Lincoln's regard for Christian institutions, great prominence is given to his proclamation to the army enjoining the observance of the Sabbath. This document gives expression to sentiments regarding the sanctity of the Christian Sabbath that Lincoln personally did not entertain. It was issued to appease the clamor of the clergy who demanded it, and was drafted, not by Lincoln, but by some pious Sabbatarian. Lincoln himself attached no more sanctity to Sunday than to other days. He worked on Sunday himself. In Springfield his Sundays were frequently spent in preparing cages for court. In company with his boys he often passed the entire day making excursions into the country or rambling through the woods that skirted the Sangamon. He seldom went to church either in Springfield or Washington, the claims of some of his Christian biographers to the contrary notwithstanding. Previous to his nomination, in 1860, we find him sitting for a bust on Sunday in preference to attending church. On the Sunday immediately following his nomination an artist was busy with him molding his hands and taking negatives for a statue. The draft of the preliminary Proclamation of Emancipation was finished on Sunday. The last Sunday of his life was spent, not in studying the Scriptures, but in reading his beloved Shakespeare.

It was stated by friends of Lincoln that he generally refrained from giving publicity to his religious opinions while in public life because of their unpopularity. In answer to this the Christian claimant retorts: "If this be true then he was a hypocrite." But let us be honest. Nearly every person entertains opinions which he does not deem it discreet or necessary to make public. You, my Christian friend, entertain doubts and heresies concerning your creed which you keep a secret or disclose only to your most intimate associates. If you, in private life, and not dependent upon the public, hide your unpopular thoughts from the world, can you consistently blame Lincoln for his silence when the fate of a nation depended upon him and the alienation even of a few bigots might turn the scales against him? A Christian general does not hesitate to deceive the enemy or withhold his plans even from his own soldiers. Again, the clergy are forever advising and entreating men not to publish their doubts and heresies. Is it consistent in them to condemn a man for following their advice?

The church should learn to respect honesty herself before she charges others with dishonesty. It is the shame of Christianity that men have been obliged to conceal their honest convictions in order to escape ostracism and persecution. When the church herself becomes honest enough to tolerate and respect the honest opinions of those who cannot conscientiously accept her creed, then will it be time for her to charge Lincoln with hypocrisy for having partially withheld his unpopular views from religious ruffians. It does not evince a want of honesty, nor even a lack of moral courage, to flee from a tiger or avoid a skunk.

To do good was Lincoln's religion. To live an honest, manly life to add to the sum of human happiness to make the world better for his having lived – this was the aspiration of his life and the essence of his faith.

In youth, the meanest creature found in him a friend, and if need be, a defender. He wrote essays and made speeches against cruelty to animals, and sought to impress upon his playmates' minds the sacredness of life. The same tender regard for the weak and unfortunate characterized his manhood. Whilst riding through a forest once with a party of friends, he saw a brood of young birds on the ground which a storm had blown from their nest. He dismounted from his horse, and after a laborious search, found the nest and placed the birdlings snugly in their little home. When he reached his companions, and was chided by them for his delay, he said: "I could not have slept to-night if I had not given those birds to their mother."

The narration of his many deeds of kindness and mercy while at Washington would fill a volume. He loved to rescue an erring soldier boy from the jaws of death and fill a mother's eyes with tears of joy. He loved to dispel the clouds of sorrow from a wife's sad heart and warm it with the sunshine of happiness. He loved to take the child of poverty upon his knee and plant within its little breast the seeds of confidence and hope.

A giant in stature, and a lion in strength and courage, he possessed the gentleness of a child and the tenderness of a woman. The sufferings, even of a stranger, would fill his eyes with tears, and the death of a friend would overwhelm him. In his tenth year his mother died, and for a time his heart was desolate and he could not be consoled. In his fifteenth year his only sister, a lovely, fragile flower, just blooming into womanhood, drooped and died, and life seemed purposeless to him again. Of his four children, two died while he was living – Eddie, a fair-haired babe, and his beloved Willie. When death took these his sorrow was unutterable. The untimely death of his young friend, the gallant Colonel Ellsworth, at Alexandria, and the death of his life-long friend, the lamented Edwin F. Baker, at Ball's Bluff, were blows that staggered him. At the death of his good friend, Bowlin Green, he was chosen to deliver a funeral address. When the hour arrived, and he stepped forward to perform the sacred task, his eyes fell upon the coffin of his dead friend and for a time he stood transfixed helpless and speechless. The only tribute he could pay was the tribute of his tears. When he turned for the last time from the bedside of the beautiful Ann Rutledge, his be-trothed, it was with a broken heart and a mind dethroned. "Oh! I can never be reconciled to have the snow, the rain, and the storm beat upon her grave," was the pitiful burden of his plaint for weeks. Reason after a time returned, but his wonted gladness never; and down through all those eventful years to that fatal April night when his own sweet life-blood slowly oozed away, beneath that sparkling surface of feigned mirth, drifted the memory and the agonies of that great grief.

In the social relations of life, he was a most exemplary man. He was a devoted husband, an indulgent father, an obliging neighbor, and a faithful friend. Mrs. Colonel Chapman, a lady who lived for a time in his family, pays this tribute to his private life: "He was all that a husband, father, and neighbor should be, kind and affectionate to his wife and child, and very pleasant to all around him. Never did I hear him utter an unkind word."

"His devotion to wife and children," says George W. Julian, "was as abiding and unbounded as his love of country." The strong attachment always manifested by him for his friends has often been remarked. Rich and poor, great and humble, all were equally dear to him and alike the recipients of his regard and love. The prince he treated like a man, the humblest man he treated like a prince. Nothing in his career exhibits the greatness and nobleness of his character in a loftier degree than the cordial and unaffected manner in which, at Washington, in the midst of wealth, and splendor, and refinement, he was accustomed to receive and entertain the plain, uncultured friends of other days.

Upon his rugged honesty, I need not dwell. The *sobriquet* of "Honest Abe" was early won by him and never lost. In his profession – a profession in which, too often, cunning and deceit, falsehood and dishonesty, are the means, and robbery the end – a profession in which, too often, Injustice is a purpled Dives sitting at a bounteous board, and Justice, a ragged Lazarus lying at the gate – he never wavered in his loyalty to truth, to justice, and to honesty. Engaged in a just cause, he was one of the most powerful advocates that ever addressed a judge or jury; engaged in an unjust cause, he was the weakest member of his bar. In fact, he could not be induced to plead a cause in which he did not see some element of justice, even though the technicalities of law insured success. To one who had sought his services and had stated his case, he replied: "Yes, I can win it; but there are some things *legally* right that are not *morally* right; this is one: I cannot take your case." He was once employed to defend a person accused of murder. As the trial progressed, it became apparent to him that his client had done the deed. Turning to his associate counsel, with a look of disappointment and pain, he said: "Swett, the man is guilty; you defend him; I cannot." On another occasion, when he discovered that his client had grossly imposed upon his confidence and instituted an unjust suit, he left the court-room, and when the bailiff called for him, he answered

"Tell Judge Treat that I can't come; *I have to wash my hands.*"
He was the most magnanimous of men. William H. Seward, his chief opponent for the Presidential nomination, he made the Premier of his Cabinet. Secretary Chase became his political, if not his personal, enemy. Yet, recognizing his fitness for the place, he waived all personal grievances and appointed him to the exalted position of Chief Justice of the United States, the highest gift within the power of a President to bestow. During his professional career he was sent to Cincinnati to assist Edwin M. Stanton in an important legal case. The grim Stanton had never met this plain, Western lawyer before, and displeased at his uncouth appearance, and apparent lack of ability, treated him so discourteously that Lincoln's self-respect compelled him to practically withdraw from the case. It was a brutal affront, too poignant for him ever to forget, but not to forgive, and linked together on one of the most momentous pages of history stand the names of Lincoln and Stanton, an enduring witness to his sublime magnanimity.

The murder of this loving savior of our Union was a disastrous blow, not to the victorious North alone, but to the vanquished South as well. Could he have lived, the balm of his great, kindly nature would have quickly healed the nation's wounds. At the commencement of the conflict, in pleading tones, he said: "We are not enemies, but friends." And at its close, notwithstanding all the cruel, bitter anguish he had endured during those four long years of fratricidal strife, "With malice toward none, with charity for all," he died, and many a brave Confederate deplored "The deep damnation of his taking off." When Stonewall Jackson died, he paid a touching tribute to his gallantry, and said: "Let us forget his errors over his fresh-made grave." In the darkness of night, on a bloody field of the Peninsula, he bent beside the prostrate form of a dying soldier of the South, and while the hot tears rolled down his furrowed cheeks, soothed him with words of tenderest sympathy, and, by the dim rays of a lantern, took down from his lips a message to his mother, and sent it by a flag of truce into the enemies' lines to be transmitted to his home.

Glorious apostle of humanity! When shall we look upon his like again? so honest, so truthful, so just, so charitable, so loving, so merciful? Law was his God, justice his creed, and liberty his heaven. If he sinned, mercy prompted him. In the presence of such a man, and in the presence of such a religion, how contemptible your puny theologians and their narrow creeds appear! Born in the cabin of a Western wild, dying in a nation's capital, its honored chief, enshrined in the hearts of an admiring world, Abraham Lincoln stands to-day the gentlest, purest, noblest character in human history. Millenniums may pass away, unnumbered generations come and go, creeds rise and fall; but the divine faith of Freedom's martyr – a faith based upon immutable law, eternal justice, universal liberty – a faith formulated not in perishable words, but in immortal deeds, will live through all the years to come, a torch of hope to every son of toil.

www.ingramcontent.com/pod-product-compliance
Lightning Source LLC
Chambersburg PA
CBHW071420090426
42737CB00011B/1523